Kill Bad Meetings

Also by Kevan Hall

Speed Lead
Making the Matrix Work

Kill Bad Meetings

Cut 50% of your meetings to transform
your culture, improve collaboration,
and accelerate decisions

KEVAN HALL and ALAN HALL

NICHOLAS BREALEY
PUBLISHING
London • Boston

First published in 2017 by Nicholas Brealey Publishing
An imprint of John Murray Press

An Hachette UK company

1

British Library Cataloguing-in-Publication Data
A catalogue record for this book is available from the British Library.

Hardback ISBN 978-1-47366-837-9
Trade paperback ISBN 978-1-47366-835-5
eBook (UK) ISBN 978-1-47366-836-2
eBook (US) ISBN 978-1-47366-843-0

Typeset by Hewer Text UK Ltd, Edinburgh
Printed and bound by Clays Ltd, St Ives plc

John Murray Press policy is to use papers that are natural, renewable and
recyclable products and made from wood grown in sustainable forests.
The logging and manufacturing processes are expected to conform
to the environmental regulations of the country of origin.

Nicholas Brealey Publishing
John Murray Press
Carmelite House
50 Victoria Embankment
London, EC4Y 0DZ, UK
Tel: 020 3122 6000

Nicholas Brealey Publishing
Hachette Book Group
Market Place Center,
53 State Street
Boston, MA 02109, USA
Tel: (617) 263 1834

www.nicholasbrealey.com
www.killbadmeetings.com

To family and freedom

Acknowledgements

Many people contributed to the contents of this book, particularly our principal colleagues at Global Integration: Tony Poots, Phil Stockbridge, John Bland, Rod Farnan, Joff Marshall-Lee, T.H. Ong, and Robyn Green. They develop, apply, and improve these ideas every month in dozens of face-to-face and online training programs.

Thank you to our central support team who make sure our materials and programs get sold, produced, delivered, and paid for by new and existing clients globally, both online and in person.

Thank you to our many clients and the tens of thousands of participants on our training programs around the world, for challenging and improving these concepts and tools and keeping us focused on the practical applications to their real world. Only the things that really worked survived to be in the book.

Thanks also to all at Nicholas Brealey Publishing for helping us shape our ideas and share them with a wider population.

Contents

CONTENTS

Preface

How would you like to save a day a week by cutting out completely unnecessary work?

You already suspect that half of what happens in meetings is not relevant or useful. Even the useful meetings are often badly run, do not meet their planned outcomes, and lack participation.

Despite this it is hard to persuade others to let you escape or to change the way meetings run.

This book will help you identify and disconnect from the 50 percent of unnecessary topics and meetings and improve the ones that remain to make them more effective, relevant, and engaging.

It will only cost you the time you need to read this book and apply some of the practical ideas you will find here. It could be the best investment in your productivity and engagement that you ever make.

Meetings are essential to any organization. They are where we collaborate and make decisions, and where we spend an average of two days per week of our time – or over 15 years of our working lives.

Unfortunately, meetings are often unnecessary or badly run.

- Up to half of the content of meetings is either not relevant to participants or could be delivered more simply outside a meeting
- Up to 20 percent of meeting participants should not be there
- Up to 40 percent of meeting time is spent sharing information that could be delivered before the meeting
- The meetings that do need to happen often fail to deliver their outcomes effectively and lack opportunities to participate

We have spent the last 20 years working with increasingly complex teams and organizations. Most were virtual or global, many operating in complex matrix or network organization structures.

Collaboration in these and most other companies has become more widespread and more complex. Work increasingly cuts across the traditional silos to include colleagues from other functions, business units, and geographies. We struggle to be effective as members of multiple teams, working for multiple bosses, and engaging with a diverse network of colleagues and stakeholders.

Yet, as we work with these increasingly complex groups of people, time and again we find that the challenge comes back to meetings. Meetings are where collaboration happens, where decisions get made, and where people spend a lot of their least favorite time. People are frustrated with too many boring, irrelevant, or badly run meetings.

If we can fix the way we meet, which is a very tangible and achievable goal, we can have a huge impact on effectiveness, collaboration, and decision-making.

Kevan is an experienced line manager, CEO, and consultant whose previous books *Speed Lead* and *Making the Matrix Work* focused on getting things done more effectively in complex organizations. His consulting and training work has given him a broad view of meetings cultures in many of the world's leading organizations.

Alan also knows about life in large organizations having worked in the packaged goods industry, most recently as a national account manager managing the relationship between the world's largest food company and the UK's largest retailer. He brings the perspective of a Generation Y/millennial working through the challenges of management and meetings and questioning why it needs to be this way.

This book is focused on practical steps you can take to improve meetings. Where we have reduced the number and improved the quality of face-to-face and virtual meetings, we have seen significant improvements in collaboration, speed of decision-making, and employee engagement, as well as major reductions in cost.

Today meetings consume about 40 percent of working time for managers and professional people (our most expensive people).

- Our research shows that managerial and professional people on average spend two days per week in meetings
- Bain and Company studied the time budgets of 17 organizations in detail and found that, on average, senior leaders devote two days a week to meetings and 15 percent of an organization's collective time is spent in meetings
- A 2012 survey by salary.com found "too many meetings" to be the number one time-waster at the office, with 47 percent of votes, up from number three in 2008

For organizations, this is a huge cost. The typical managerial or professional person in Europe or the USA costs around $100,000 to employ (at 2017 prices). Some $40,000 of this is spent directly in attending meetings. Preparation for meetings is in addition to this, and internal meetings are also a major driver of business travel costs.

Because the salaries and expenses of people who prepare for and travel to meetings are spread across the whole organization the total cost of these meetings is often not visible.

One of our clients with 80,000 people worldwide calculated that the cost of unnecessary meeting attendance alone was $500 million per year and this drove an additional $400 million of travel costs. If we add in an assumption for preparation time, then we are looking at over $1 billion of wasted cost every year for just that one organization.

We may have full-time professionals managing budgets or spends of a tiny fraction of this, but anyone can call, run, and attend meetings just about whenever they want. The same individual who would need to get approval from three managers for their $200 flight can happily spend $40,000 per year of their time in meetings.

Meetings are probably the largest unmanaged cost area in large organizations.

A 2016 *Harvard Business Review* article, "Collaborative Overload" by Cross, Rebele, and Grant, claims that over the last 20 years the time spent by people in collaborative activities (meetings, calls, emails etc.) has increased by 50 percent or more and can take up 80 percent of the week for many employees – leaving little time for other work.

In this article the authors identify that the collaborative load falls most heavily on a small number of high performers. In most cases 20–35 percent of value-added collaborations came from only 3–5 percent of employees.

Worryingly, the study also finds that the people who are the best sources of information and in highest demand as collaborators have the lowest engagement and career satisfaction scores, which can lead to their leaving, or becoming apathetic, or less effective.

Too much collaboration can drive your best people away. It also makes you wonder what the rest of the people are doing in these meetings.

As products and services become more complex and organizations become increasingly connected, the need for more collaborative work increases. At the same time as we need to be more connected, we also need to be effective and productive – we can't afford to spend our whole time in meetings, conference calls, video, or web conferences.

Technology is turning out to be a mixed blessing in our meetings. There is no doubt that virtual meetings reduce costs and make communication with remote colleagues easier. Video and web conferencing tools have reduced the cost of travel and time away from the office.

However, reducing cost and improving ease of use have led to more meetings in total. It is much easier for a manager with a virtual or global team to call a quick video or web conference than to arrange a face-to-face meeting – so they do it more often.

Open-plan offices mean that it is far easier to walk up and interrupt someone and bring them into an ad hoc discussion or meeting. New office buildings are actively designed to encourage communication and provide areas for spontaneous meetings.

Because these types of meetings are more common and more spontaneous they can offer real value; however, they are also usually less well-planned and can be time-consuming.

At the same time as the number of meetings is increasing, there is a great deal of dissatisfaction about the quality and relevance of those meetings.

- 4,000 participants in our training programs tell us that of the two days per week they spend in meetings only half of it is relevant and necessary for them to do their jobs
- In the Bain study of 17 large corporations, leaders said that half of the meetings they go to are "ineffective" or "very ineffective"

Virtual meetings bring additional challenges in creating participation and engagement. In many cases, people have used these tools to bring boring "page turning" PowerPoint monologues at lower cost to a more distributed and uninterested audience.

Dissatisfaction with meetings is nothing new but, as the number of meetings increases, this becomes a very significant cost.

- At corporate level, it means that our people are spending a day per week in unnecessary meetings – an average of $20,000 waste per managerial or professional employee every year
- At an individual level, it means busy individuals are frustrated and disengaged at having to spend a day a week doing completely unnecessary work – this adds up to each of us wasting eight years or more of our working lives

It is hard to imagine any other area of business where we would accept such high levels of waste. Imagine building a new factory where 50 percent of everything we made was scrap and had to be thrown away. Imagine trying to get approval for a new product that only worked half of the time. Both these are laughable and we would probably be fired for suggesting them. However, 50 percent waste is normal and accepted in our meetings.

In a business climate where we all need to do more with less, where people claim to be more and more busy and where productivity improvement remains a challenge for all organizations, the opportunity to win back 20 percent of the time for our most valuable and expensive people should surely be a priority.

We acknowledge that many meetings are relevant and some are even well run. There is good evidence that face-to-face meetings with customers, for example, are a good investment. When we are building relationships, collaborating creatively, and dealing with sensitive issues, then a meeting makes sense.

We also recognize that individuals attend meetings for many other reasons than just getting the work done. Even the worst meetings can have valuable by-products like learning, networking, and visibility. As we cut out unnecessary meetings we will need to find better ways to deliver these valuable outcomes.

We have been looking so far at the rational arguments, the cost, and the waste; there is also an emotional argument based around the frustration and stupidity of creating unnecessary work.

We are sure most of you already have experiences of meetings that are just ridiculous. Here is one from Kevan's corporate career in the days before he had the language and the techniques to push back successfully.

I was working on a project in Eastern Europe and reported functionally into human resources. I was really busy, travelling on average to three countries a week and living with my family in France.

The European HR head asked me to attend his monthly "team meeting" in the UK. I explained that I had a very high workload already, that the content of the meeting did not really have any relevance to me, and that I could do without another international trip. I asked if I could stay out of the meeting.

He responded that he wanted me to be part of the team and, even though I explained that I did not really collaborate with any other of the attendees and did not need to, he insisted I attend.

So, I left home very early in the morning to take a 90-minute drive to the airport for a one-hour flight and another 45-minute taxi journey to the UK office to arrive by 9 a.m.

The first item on the agenda was a compensation and benefits review. If you have never sat through one of these before, they are extremely dull (unless of course it is your own compensation). The topic was not relevant to me at all and it looked like it would take a while, so I quietly started to do my emails.

My boss asked me to step outside the meeting and asked me what I was doing. I explained that I was busy and that I did not think the topic was relevant to me or that I had anything to contribute. I asked if I could step out.

He became quite angry and insisted that I was not showing respect to the team. I tried to explain again that I was not really part of the team because I did not collaborate with anyone there but he insisted I should re-join the meeting and "look interested."

I tried to look interested but the topic was boring and was not relevant. Soon my face started to hurt.

To keep engaged I began to ask questions. Remember, these are questions that I do not need to know the answer to. The compensation and benefits specialist now had to waste his time and that of everybody else in the meeting answering these very basic questions.

Ten minutes later, as an experienced manager, I started to warm to the discussion and began to generate ideas. These ideas, based on a full ten minutes' experience, were not very good. The whole meeting now had to take time to discuss and deal with these ideas. None of them advanced the topic noticeably.

After an hour, the compensation and benefits specialist made a recommendation. At this point, there was one special- ist in the room who really knew what he was talking about and 14 generalists, including myself, who generally did not.

When the process for taking a decision on the recommen- dation was to take a vote, I realized that my opinion, based on one hour of disinterested observation, was just as valuable as a career of specialist experience.

The compensation and benefits specialist was not very happy with the outcome of the vote. He knew that the recom- mendation was wrong and, as he was responsible for imple- menting it, he would have to find a way to change the decision after the meeting.

The meeting continued in similar style for a full day. I was invited to continue to attend that meeting every month for the *following 18 months. I managed to find urgent business reasons for missing as many as possible but it was still two weeks of my life I will never get back.*

When we tell this story to participants on our training programs, they laugh. Then we ask, when was the last time you were in a meeting just like this one? Most answer – in the last week!

Later in the book we will unpick many of the issues in this meeting, from finding unnecessary participants and topics to improving the relevance and decision processes.

There is a saying in marketing, *"Half my advertising is wasted, I just do not know which half"* (attributed to John Wannamaker among others). The good news about meetings is that we *do* know which half is wasted and in this book we will show you how to cut out the unnecessary meetings, topics, and participants that make many meetings irrelevant.

Once we cut out these completely unnecessary meetings and topics, we will move on to focus on improving the planning and running of the remaining 50 percent of meetings that do need to happen. Even relevant meetings often suffer from poor design, lack of participation, unclear outcomes, too much information-sharing, and slow decision-making.

If you are new to running meetings virtually or globally you may also need to develop some new skills and techniques. If you are running large events and conferences, the costs and opportunities are even larger.

Many organizations have tried to improve their meetings by focusing solely on improving facilitation and the conduct of their meetings. This does help, but an essential first step is to cut out the meetings that do not need to happen in the first place

– otherwise we are just training people to be more efficient at managing work that does not need to be done.

Meetings training also tends to focus on the individual facilitator or chairperson. These are important roles but they comprise the minority of attendees at the meeting. We will also focus on the role of the participants. If we have one chairperson and 12 participants, then the participant experience and the relevance of the content to them is a major factor in both the cost of and satisfaction with the meeting.

Improving meetings is more than just giving people new knowledge or skills. If we ask people in focus groups and interviews to tell us how to run the perfect meeting most of them can already give a good answer. They already know how to run a good meeting, but they tell us they rarely attend meetings that are run this way.

We have learned that improving meetings is about more than just training. Training tends to give an individual the skills and motivation to make a change, but it is hard for them to systematically change the meeting culture of their organization.

We need something more systematic across the whole organization which addresses not only the symptoms of too many meetings but the underlying corporate cultural causes and the resistance to change in ways of working.

In this book:

- We will show you how to put together a business case to build commitment to change and gain resources to support the introduction of new ways of meeting
- We will help you understand and deal with the underlying corporate cultural drivers of your meetings culture

- We will introduce some practical actions and steps to significantly reduce the number of your meetings by cutting out unnecessary meetings, topics, and participants
- We will show you how to design more effective virtual and face-to-face meetings using our OPPT framework, including how to improve participation, speed up decision-making, and reduce the amount of information-sharing
- We will look specifically at the added challenges of running virtual and international meetings and large events more effectively
- We will show you how to make your meeting flow better, through improved facilitation and continuous improvement
- We will help you embed the change and overcome resistance to introducing new ways of working

A millennial perspective

Most researchers define millennials as people born between the early 1980s until the late 1990s or early 2000s. They have distinct preferences that are already influencing how we will need to meet in the future.

Millennials are no longer just the new kids on the block or the latest consumer marketing segment. They are now our professionals, first line managers, and increasingly our middle managers. By 2020 they will be more than 50 percent of the global workforce.

It is always dangerous to stereotype; for example it is clear that the life experiences and priorities of an 18-year-old student in rural China are rather different from those of a 30-year-old manager with a mortgage and a family to support in London.

We believe that, despite the host of articles and blogs detailing the uniqueness of Generation Y or millennials, a lot of the differences are largely attributable to the normal progression of life stages and the variety of life experiences.

LIFE STAGES CREATE COMMON PERSPECTIVES
- Young people, quite properly, undervalue experience and hierarchy (because they do not have them) and older people typically undervalue youth and energy (because they may have lost them)
- People early in their careers are inevitably frustrated with the pace of development, the hierarchies they are not part of and the speed of personal and professional progress
- Mobility is higher in younger people who often have fewer commitments and this may be reflected in lower organizational loyalty
- More established managers who have earned their position through long experience and hard work may be frustrated as younger people want to leapfrog above them

These are nothing new.

LIFE EXPERIENCES DIFFER, INCLUDING
- Whether you first moved into work during a relative boom or during a recession
- Which culture or economic group you were brought up in
- Your educational background

These factors can vary widely for individuals within the millennial generation and the other generations before them.

They are nothing new either.

In a book targeted at a global audience we should recognize that there will be tremendous variety in people born within any arbitrary set of dates.

At worst, some of the writing about millennials sounds like the age-old complaints about "the youth of today" not being "like us." This has led to reports claiming that millennials are over-entitled, self-focused, and even narcissistic.

Even if it were possible to stereotype half of the working population of the world it would not be particularly helpful so we shall avoid over-generalizing.

We do, however, intend to reflect the energy and positive force for change that youth can bring. We look to develop new ways of working that will make things better for all the generations currently at work – and for the next ones coming through including generations Z, Alpha, and beyond.

So what is really different?

1. Technology

Millennials do have a fundamentally different attitude toward the use of technology and we will reflect that in this book.

People who have always known the Internet and the easy availability of communication and social collaboration tools expect fast access to information; they naturally reach out to an extended network to reinforce their learning and to gather information and support.

They are used to instantly downloading effective communication and collaboration tools on a free app, rather than waiting for two years for corporate IT to evaluate a secure and support-able new tool.

The idea of needing to wait for a week to book time in a video conference suite to connect with colleagues seems bizarre to those brought up with FaceTime and Skype.

Why would you wait for a month until the next meeting when you can instant message the relevant person with the expertise and get a response straightaway?

More than 40 percent of over 4,000 graduates across 75 coun-tries in research by Opinium Research for PWC in 2011 felt that "their use of technology was not always understood," and 65 percent felt held back by rigid hierarchies and outdated manage-ment and working styles. Millennials in Africa were the most likely to feel this way.

Learning to integrate new technologies into the way we work gives fantastic opportunities for improving productivity and engagement. Social tools will help support remote working and build a sense of community in distributed organizations. Communication and collaboration technologies can help us work more effectively, particularly when we are working with colleagues in different locations.

There is mixed research about millennials' preferences for face-to-face versus virtual communication. Some researchers claim that they prefer a more collegiate, face-to-face way of working and others that they are much more comfortable with communicating through technology.

We believe that these views are not incompatible. Indeed, people who have grown up with access to the Internet, social media, and easy online communication are much more comfortable with transactional or "shallow" social contact. However, at an early stage in their career they understand deeply the need for networking, visibility, and learning through face-to-face interactions.

2. Expectations of participation

The Internet means that millennials are used to a richer, multimedia way of learning and working. If you want to find out something you can rapidly locate a YouTube video about it, browse several articles, join a conversation and get immediate access to people with a point of view. Unsurprisingly, they are not as accepting of one-way lectures and boring presentations.

Millennials in many parts of the world have been brought up in a more participative way than previous generations, they have been more involved in family decisions, and according to some researchers are more supported by and more connected to parents than previous generations.

They are used to joining conversations and having their opinions heard and responded to.

They bring this perspective to business meetings, expecting to be involved and engaged. This energy, we hope, will improve meetings for everybody and we will make some recommendations on how to make meetings much more participative and engaging.

As they move into work, people who have been used to instant responses, likes, and tweets bring a preference for very regular feedback, mentoring, and working with experienced people from whom they can learn. These are all good practices in developing and motivating people, irrespective of age.

Some organizations are now using reverse mentoring, where a younger manager is paired with a more experienced one. The younger person learns more about management, the older more about technology – everybody wins.

3. Interest in the wider world

Seventy-one percent of millennials in the PWC survey were keen to have an international move at some stage during their career.

Even those who do not go to live and work in another culture will find that international collaboration becomes the norm as organizations become more integrated, virtual, matrixed, and global. The content of this book explicitly deals with the international and virtual dimensions of meetings.

During the rest of the book we are not going to comment constantly on millennial perspectives as separate and different; instead we are going to marry good practice from leading organizations with the stimulus and perspective of a technology-enabled, participative, and internationally connected generation to develop new meeting practices that are even better for everyone and for the businesses we all work in.

There were, however, a couple of areas where we disagreed quite strongly and had to work hard to find ways to reconcile our different views; these will become evident later.

The practical tools and techniques you will find in the following chapters come from our experiences training tens of thousands of participants from major organizations around the world. We develop new ideas based on our own and external research, we test them with participants, and we regularly attend business meetings to observe and improve the way these meetings work. What survives this process are real-world techniques that can make a significant difference to the number and quality of your meetings.

If you follow the actions and targets in this book you should be able to save yourself at least a day per week of unnecessary meetings and radically improve the ones that remain.

If you need more help with implementing this approach in your organization, you can find out more about how we can help through consulting, training, and online learning at the end of the book.

Good luck.

Kevan Hall and Alan Hall
meetings@global-integration.com
www.global-integration.com
@killbadmeetings

PART 1

The opportunities and barriers to fewer, better meetings

• • •

In the Preface we outlined at a high level the cost of meetings to organizations in general.

In Part 1 we will show you how to identify the real cost of meetings in your specific organization and how to use this to build the business case for change and for investment in improving your meetings.

Although the principles that follow are relatively simple, it can be surprisingly hard to change your meetings culture. This is because having too many meetings is often a symptom of some deeper underlying corporate cultural beliefs and practices.

We will help you to understand and find ways of dealing with these underlying problems to sustain your move to fewer, better meetings.

Chapter 1

The best business case you never made

 Actions – put together a business case for improving meetings in your organization

 Target – raise your own and your organization's awareness of the cost of meetings and the opportunity to improve

As we have already seen in the Preface, the total cost of meetings to organizations in general is huge.

However, in building a business case and being credible in proposing change, we need to be specific about the impact on our own organization. While many people think they attend too many meetings, the total cost of these meetings is often hidden in individual budgets and the salaries and expense budgets of those who attend.

It is tempting to jump right in and try to improve your meetings but we have found it to be essential to put together a proper business case for four key reasons:

1. The numbers are usually startling and this can help build the energy and the desire to change
2. It requires quite significant effort to change our culture around meetings. We are not going to achieve this just by running a few meetings training sessions, so we need to build a proper business foundation for the investment and effort involved
3. If we are going to get priority for this initiative, we need to be able to see a significant payback. Think of this project as similar in scale and return to opening a new office, launching a significant new product or service, or massively improving the performance of a factory. Imagine yourself pitching for investment at this level
4. Any quality improvement exercise should start with a measure. Start by calculating the cost and quality of your meetings and raising awareness with your colleagues. This will also give you a "before" measure against which to evaluate the success of your changes

Luckily this information about meetings is not hard to find.

The costs of meetings fall into two categories: direct costs and consequent costs.

For the purposes of this book we will define "meetings" as including more than two people either face to face or through technology – conference call, video, or web meeting. We exclude one-to-one meetings as many of the principles later in the book will not apply to these conversations.

In this chapter, we will use examples at an organizational level; you can also take these principles to put together a business case just for your own meeting or at a departmental level.

Direct costs

Direct costs include:

- The salary costs of attendees
- The salary costs of preparation and travel
- The expenses involved in running the meeting

These are relatively easy to find.

1. Salary costs of attendees

First, find the number of people in your organization who are regularly attending meetings. Most people attend some meetings, but the real problems and opportunities for improvement are likely to be among your managerial and professional populations. This will often be the top 10–15 percent of people in your organization (depending on your industry and business).

Almost everyone attends some meetings but you will get most benefit by keeping it simple and focused on this more senior group. They are also the people who drive the meetings attended by most of the rest. If you can change the way they work the approach will trickle down as they realize the benefits and change their behaviors around meetings. This way you will influence everyone else too.

Second, calculate the average cost of these people. Your payroll or HR people will have this information.

We know from our own research that the average cost of employment (salary, social charges, and other direct costs of employment) of a manager or professional person in Europe or the USA is about $100,000 (at 2017 rates). It is worth finding out the actual figure for your business – for several of our clients' their corporate average for these populations has been above $200,000.

Third, ask your people two simple questions:

Think about the meetings you attend where there are more than two people present – whether that is face to face or virtual (audio, video, or web meetings).
1. *How much of your time on average do you spend in these meetings?*
2. *Of that time, what percentage of the meeting is relevant to you – that is, you need to be there to do your job?*

Our survey of over 4,000 people working in complex organizations tells us that the average is 40 percent of time in meetings and only 50 percent of that time is relevant.

Other sources confirm this as being in the right ballpark.

- A *Harvard Business Review* article in 2014, "Your Scarcest Resource," found that on average senior executives spent more than two days per week in meetings. Fifteen percent of an organization's collective time is spent in meetings, a percentage that has increased every year since 2008
- The *Wall Street Journal* found that senior executives were spending 40 percent of a 55-hour work week in meetings and calls
- A 2005 Microsoft survey found that 69 percent of people feel meetings aren't productive

- Studies by Atlassian found that employees considered 50 percent of the time they spent in meetings was wasted

With a group of individuals, you will find a very wide range of answers to the first question with some people claiming 10 percent or less of their time is spent in meetings and others, particularly middle or senior managers, spending over 80 percent of their time there.

The answer to the second question generally depends on the answer to the first. People who have very few meetings usually think they are very relevant; people who have a lot of meetings usually think that relevance is lower.

The problem is usually greater at senior levels where the costs are significantly higher, they attend more meetings, and the relevance is lower.

You can do this easily through an online survey or through interviews or focus groups. If you need support with this or putting together your business case, we have existing formats and surveys available and offer consulting in this area. You will find our contact details at the end of this book.

Worked example
- A client of ours with 50,000 employees found 7,000 of these were regularly involved in meetings
- The average salary cost of these individuals was $100,000 per year
- They spent on average 46 percent of their time in meetings and only 48 percent of the content was relevant. This meant that 24 percent of their time was spent in unnecessary meetings

Taking these points together, this meant that the salary cost of unnecessary meeting **attendance alone** each year was **$168 million per year.**

If that figure looks far too high to you, do the analysis for your own organization; most people are surprised the first time they calculate this largely hidden cost.

2. Salary costs of preparation and travel

A 2014 *Harvard Business Review* article analyzed how much time was spent supporting a weekly executive committee meeting.

- The weekly executive committee meeting directly consumed 7,000 hours of executive time per year, already a lot
- To prepare for this the 11 attendees each held (level 1) preparation meetings consuming another 20,000 hours
- To prepare for these the attendees also called their own (level 2) preparation meetings in turn
- In total the single executive committee meeting consumed 300,000 hours of work every year

Source: Michael C. Mankins, "This Weekly Meeting Took Up 300,000 Hours a Year," *HBR,* 2014

If we apply our average cost of $100,000 per person per year to these figures, then this one meeting is generating $15 million per year of preparation cost.

In this case the amount of time spent on preparation was **over 40 times** the time spent in the meetings.

We did a similar exercise with a famously micromanaging CEO of a financial services organization. His weekly meetings asked inappropriately detailed questions of senior leaders, expecting them to know what every office had sold the previous week. We calculated that over 10,000 people had to submit at least some input to make sure all the business heads were (over) prepared, every week.

You can get this information by using surveys, focus groups, and interviews with people who attend meetings to look at how they and their people prepare.

If you choose a high-profile meeting like an executive committee, regional leadership team, or global marketing or other functional group you will start to see some very large figures.

If you want a very rough and very conservative assumption for your business case, you can assume that the cost of preparation is **at the very least** the same as the cost of the salary of people attending. This is likely to significantly undervalue the real cost of preparation but stops people claiming that you are over-estimating the costs.

If you have accurate data from your own survey, interviews, or focus groups, of course, then include this instead.

Travel time is a major source of cost for international meetings. It can take a whole day to fly to attend even a short meeting. For transatlantic meetings, you often waste a day getting there and maybe even a day getting back depending on the time zones. If this is your reality, do not forget to include some estimate of the time for this in your business case.

Even a short amount of travel can quickly add up. For anyone spending 30 minutes to travel to a one-hour meeting, the round-trip travel takes as long as the meeting.

Of course, we have many more opportunities to meet virtually these days and these tools can significantly reduce travel time.

3. Expenses involved in running the meeting

This is an important category and, particularly for international businesses, can be nearly as expensive as the cost of wasted time.

This will normally include:

- The costs of providing space or renting a meeting room
- Attendance expenses – including travel, accommodation, and meals

You should be able to get this information from your finance department or from looking at your own budgets. If you can halve the frequency of your meetings you can make a significant impact on this spend.

The cost of one person attending a two-day meeting that needs a transatlantic business-class flight plus ground transportation, hotels, and meals can easily exceed $10,000.

When you put together the direct costs of salary, preparation, and expenses, you normally have all the justification you need to invest in the change.

The client in our worked example with 7,000 regular meeting attendees estimated their cost of unnecessary meetings at:

- Salary costs – $168 million
- Preparation – $168 million
- Expenses – $50 million

Total direct costs = $386 million per year.

There is no doubt that the availability of relatively inexpensive video and web conferencing gives us a great opportunity to reduce the cost of travel and expenses in conducting virtual meetings relative to face-to-face meetings.

However, it also seems that as people find it easier to meet virtually and the cost of these meetings reduces, they are meeting more often. It would be a shame if the time saved on travel to meetings was just wasted on more unnecessary ones.

You will notice that, so far, we have just focused on the cost of **entirely unnecessary** meetings in this chapter. In Part 2 we will identify three simple steps you can take to kill unnecessary meetings and topics and cut out unnecessary participants.

After we have done that we will still be left with the half of meetings that **do** need to happen, but which are also often badly run. They cost as much again as these figures above. If we can make a 10 percent improvement (easily achievable) in these meetings, we have a whole additional business case we can make there. Parts 3 and 4 will help you design and run your necessary meetings better.

Consequent costs

In addition to these direct costs, meetings generate some consequent costs too. These are harder to quantify but if you want to be very rigorous about your business case you could also include consequent costs such as:

- Lost productivity: if these valuable people were not attending unnecessary meetings, what more useful outputs could they be providing? Assuming that people are employed because they are worth at least their salary, then the opportunity cost should be at least the cost of attending the unnecessary meeting

- Too much internal focus: meetings usually focus on internal issues and can take away from time dealing with the outside world – particularly in sales roles. If performance slips we can create a "circle of doom" with more and more internal meetings to review progress leaving even less time to perform
- Delays to delivery: when people are sitting in unnecessary meetings, they are not doing work to complete their activities. An 18-month project with a day per week of unnecessary meetings can easily take three or four months longer than it needed to
- Slow decision-making: a consequence of too many meetings and too many people involved is that decisions can become slow and ineffective. The cost of delays to new products, efficiency improvements, or projects can be very significant. If poor quality meetings delay the implementation of a project with $1 million in savings per year, the cost of delay is nearly $3,000 per day
- Ineffective collaboration: meetings are where collaboration happens in complex organizations; if our meetings are ineffective this will tend to slow down and reduce the quality of our collaboration
- People hate boring meetings: people nearly always claim they are too busy and yet they still have time to spend a day per week attending unnecessary meetings. Think of the impact on engagement of giving people back a day per week of their time and cutting out completely unnecessary and frustrating work

As you can see these are important areas but it is much more difficult to get objective information about the costs involved.

In our consulting work in this area we tend only to include the direct costs. Our experience is that if you start to load in these less quantifiable costs, it can undermine the power of your argument. People start to think you are stretching to make a business case and may argue with your assumptions. There is usually more than enough direct cost to make the point and to justify the intervention.

If you are putting together and presenting your business case we would recommend just mentioning these as additional benefits in passing.

HOW MUCH SHOULD YOU INVEST IN IMPROVING YOUR MEETINGS?

Our clients often ask, "What will it cost to improve our meetings?"

At the business case stage, we ask, "How much would you normally expect to invest to make this level of time and cost saving?"

Let us stick with our worked example company – the cost of their unnecessary meetings is $386 million per year. It is unlikely we could ever make our meetings perfect so we shouldn't attempt to claim all these savings. We think it is reasonable to base a business case around winning back half of this. Let's call it $193 million per year.

How much would you be prepared to invest in your business to create a $193 million per year improvement straight to your bottom line?

How would we treat a project like this in other areas of the business?

- First let's consider a marketing investment. How much would you be prepared to spend on a new product with a very high probability of generating an additional **profit** of $193 million per year?
- How much would you be prepared to invest in manufacturing or in your supply chain to reduce your manufacturing **costs** by $193 million per year?
- How many **additional people** would you need to recruit in sales and delivery to generate additional net revenue of $193 million per year?

If a product were generating $193 million of bottom-line profit per year at, let's say, a 10 percent profit margin, then you would need sales of $1.9 billion per year to achieve the same bottom-line impact.

The businesses we both worked for in our corporate careers tended to be looking for an internal rate of return of 40 percent; another way of putting this is a payback in two and a half years.

By these benchmarks, we would have been happy to spend $480 million to deliver this level of return.

However, for every company we have spoken to, that would be an unimaginable sum to invest in improving meetings. The most common response would be to laugh at the very idea. Why is this?

Perhaps we are not confident that we can deliver these savings? As people who have worked in business planning, sales, and manufacturing we can tell you that the returns on investment assumptions we make on capital and market investments are often no more than moderately educated guesses. In our experience, it is also quite rare that organizations go back and conduct a comprehensive evaluation later as to whether the promised return on investment was really delivered.

Sales and marketing investments in particular are often made on assumptions about customer acceptance, competitor response, or future market needs that are beyond our control. With internal spend in areas such as meetings we have much more chance of success because we can control the resources and the environment more closely.

It could also be that, because the cost of meetings is spread over every department and a lot of the cost hidden in salaries and time, nobody feels overall ownership for the issue.

This is why it is important to start with the business case. If we think about what we should be prepared to invest, we start to think more radically about the level of change we need and can afford to create in order to sustain these significant improvements.

We do not really expect to convince any client to spend $480 million on a meetings intervention. For the purposes of our business case let's be ambitious and ask for $50 million. If we invested $50 million and got an annual return of $175 million we would be seeing payback on our investment in less than four months. It would probably be the best business investment most companies made in the last decade.

Think about the scope of intervention we could design and deliver with a budget of $50 million. What could our example company afford to do? They could:

- Put all 7,000 people through several days of training on meeting effectiveness
- Put meeting coaches into all their high-profile meetings to embed best practice and support implementation of the principles

- Offer online meeting tools to help people plan and facilitate better virtual and face-to-face meetings
- Run a major change project or campaign with great communication and stakeholder management
- Study and change their corporate culture in ways that support the initiative
- Run a recognition and celebration project for meeting heroes
- Offer a prize of $1 million to the team that improved the most!

They would still be struggling to spend $10 million.

If sustainable change can be achieved with these much smaller investments, why have we taken the time to focus on such big numbers? There are three main reasons at this stage:

- Sustainably reducing the number and improving the quality of your meetings is still a major change project, not just a matter of a few workshops, so we should resource it accordingly
- Budget is a signal of intent. If your marketing head or manufacturing director came to your executive committee and offered to save $150 million per year by spending $10 million would they be believed? Would this even be worth discussing at your executive committee meeting? If the marketing head told you they could do it with a half-day training workshop, would this be credible?
- It properly positions your campaign to improve meetings as a major saving opportunity and as something that requires significant resources and leadership attention

If you really want to kill unnecessary meetings and improve the quality of the ones that remain, do the business case first and be ambitious in the scope of intervention you plan. You won't make a change in this pervasive challenge just by running a few meetings facilitation training courses; it is a significant change process.

If you can build understanding among your stakeholders of the scope of the change and invest accordingly, then you have a real chance of radically improving the effectiveness and work experience of your people and delivering significant savings to the business.

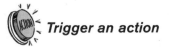 *Trigger an action*

Allocate some time in your diary to discuss this with your colleagues. Put together an outline business case for reducing the number of meetings in your business and discuss it with your key leaders or other stakeholders.

Chapter 2

The rest of the iceberg

Actions – identify the corporate cultural considerations that may be leading to too many meetings

Target – avoid resistance from your corporate culture as you begin to reduce the number of your meetings and to find alternative ways of delivering the useful by-products of ineffective meetings

It can be tempting when you identify this huge problem with your meetings to jump straight to a solution: let's improve the conduct of our meetings. While the ability to facilitate meetings well is an essential skill which we will talk about later, jumping straight to this solution usually leads to short-term improvements that soon prove unsustainable.

There are three main reasons for this:

1. Traditional meetings training doesn't address how to kill unnecessary meetings and content and cut out unnecessary participants

Unless we do this first, facilitation training just helps us to be more efficient at running meetings that do not need to happen.

In Chapters 3–5 we will look at how to eliminate unnecessary topics, meetings, and participants. Focusing the content and membership of meetings is an essential precondition to simplifying our meetings culture.

As you will see this involves challenging some of our assumptions about teamwork, involvement, and decision-making.

2. Our meetings reflect our corporate culture

If we want to sustainably reduce the number and improve the quality of our meetings we need to address some of the cultural beliefs and behaviors that drive us to meet so often.

When we work with clients in this area we try to identify:

- The deep underlying cultural drivers behind why they meet
- The artifacts and behaviors that these underlying cultural drivers create in the culture in the area of meetings
- The consequences of these artifacts and behaviors in how meetings are conducted and attended

As organizations have grown and become increasingly connected and interdependent (and in many cases more global), some of their traditional people management techniques are now either failing to work, or becoming too expensive or difficult to apply in this more complex environment.

Most of our clients are extremely well-run organizations with a legacy of strong people management techniques. Their routines, habits, and ways of working have been embedded over decades of success. These are valued and rewarded by the culture and therefore are very hard to change.

Common **deep cultural drivers** of this type include:

- A strong belief in face-to-face people management
- A belief that showing up physically equals commitment
- The importance of visibility and networking in career success and job effectiveness
- A high touch and approachable style of management
- An emphasis on creating high levels of involvement

While a lot of these are admirable, in a large complex organization these beliefs create some challenging **artifacts and behaviors,** including:

- The overuse of teams and consensus in getting things done that could be delivered faster by empowered individuals or smaller groups
- Too many people involved and consulted in meetings and decisions, leading to bureaucracy and delay
- Imprecise decision rights so it is not clear who can make decisions, how decisions are made and who needs to be involved
- Status and visibility coming from travel and attendance rather than performance

We have also often found that organizations with these beliefs tend to underinvest in communication technology. Because they overvalue face-to-face contact they may undervalue the potential usefulness of technology as an alternative. This then becomes a self-fulfilling prophecy as, if people do not have alternatives to face-to-face meetings, then the face-to-face meetings need to continue.

These artifacts and behaviors have **consequences:**

- Too many topics and participants at meetings
- Too much information-sharing
- Slow and consensus-oriented decision-making
- High levels of travel

Finally, we observe the tip of the iceberg – the symptom – too many meetings.

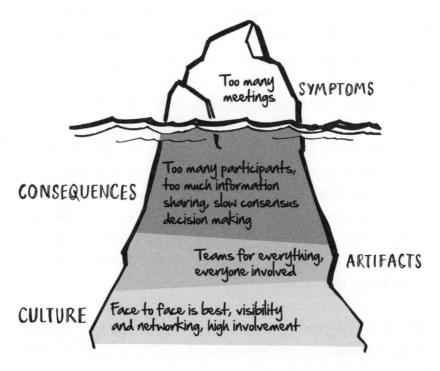

This is not to say that great companies need to abandon the deep cultural values that they hold. But they may need to find new ways to **enact** these values that are sustainable in a more complex reality.

We need to find ways to:

- Show commitment to our people without jumping on a plane, by increasing our ability to manage virtual teams and remote relationships
- Stay visible and create networks with limited face-to-face opportunities
- Generate a "high touch through hi tech" approach, integrating better use of communication and social technology
- Be more creative about involvement by doing a better job of stakeholder management and communication for those people who can't be involved in everything

If we leap straight into attacking the visible symptoms of too many meetings and we do not deal with some of the underlying dynamics, then it is likely that the corporate culture will undermine our attempts to sustainably reduce the number and improve the quality of meetings. In these conflicts, culture invariably wins.

We see a similar effect when our clients have travel freezes. Travel budgets are slashed, usually to save costs. People in the business initially complain, but often comment that they experienced fewer meetings and less interference from business visitors. In the end not travelling did not seem to make a great deal of difference. However, once the travel budget is restored, travel bounces back to the old levels.

In this case, we dealt with the symptom by just stopping travel, but we did not equip the organization with alternative tools to manage remotely, communicate through technology, and network successfully without travel. Without these alternatives, people default back to what they know and book their next flight as soon as they can.

In later chapters, we will take the time to explore some of the challenges in collaboration, involvement, and decision-making in meetings.

Because changes to meetings can challenge traditional ways of working and how you involve people, it is essential to your success that you explain **why** you are making the change and **frame this** in a way that is culturally acceptable.

This requires explaining the benefits and giving explicit permission for people to try new ways of working. It also requires the modelling of this by some of your high-profile meetings and teams – ideally your executive team.

If senior leaders and recognized high performers start to model the principles and apply them to their own meetings, then these behaviors and ways of working will start to become aspirational and valued.

If people are openly praised for joining a meeting by video conference, for example, rather than wasting time and travel expense to get face to face, then others will be encouraged to do the same.

As you introduce the changes in the following chapters, make sure to capture and celebrate success stories and recognize individuals who are trying something new.

3. Even the worst meetings can have useful by-products

"Our meetings are terrible but it is worth attending for the useful stuff we do in the breaks and evenings."

Many of us have had this experience. What was it that made the breaks and evenings so useful?

Even when our meetings are poor, people value some of the by-products, such as networking and visibility.

This was an area where we had a lively disagreement. Kevan was focused as a CEO on saving time and being more effective. Alan was passionate that, particularly in the early stages of a career, meetings were an essential opportunity to learn from others, be seen, and build contacts.

We eventually agreed that if we are going to reduce the opportunities to network and be visible in meetings, then we need to make sure we offer alternative ways of meeting these culturally useful outcomes.

It is certain that the best way to network and be visible is not sitting in an irrelevant meeting waiting for the coffee break.

With our own global team our face-to-face meetings are infrequent, no more than twice a year, so we make sure that there are regular opportunities for networking and one-to-one catch-ups both during and after the meetings.

This means not filling your meetings too full of content, finishing on time and not too late, and designing opportunities for people to work in pairs or small groups rather than always involving all meeting attendees.

If networking and visibility are the most important things, why not put them on the agenda and make them more likely to happen by regularly rotating table groups?

Well-designed social activities that encourage conversation and mixing people up can also encourage networking, but a formal dinner, a trip to the theatre or a night of go-karting may offer limited opportunities for conversation.

In Chapter 8 we will look at how to design our meetings for higher levels of participation and engagement.

Outside meetings we may need to enable more networking events or opportunities to be visible to people important to your progression and performance.

Many meetings start with a social catch-up where people share personal news and business chatter. This can be useful in developing team spirit and relationships but can make for an ineffective and slow start to meetings.

Participants who stay in touch socially between meetings either face to face or digitally report that they can begin meetings more quickly with less need for social catch-up.

If your meeting participants are physically dispersed, an internal social network or tools like Slack can provide a useful parallel social channel.

The generation now coming through into middle management has grown up with social networks and these networks can supplement other forms of discussion and meetings. However, it is essential that these platforms become part of the workflow not extra work to do on top. There needs to be a reason to interact and people across the team or business at all levels need to engage to make it work.

Used properly these tools can improve social engagement, accelerate learning, encourage group problem-solving, or ask for inputs from an extended audience.

As we replace meetings we need to look for ways to deliver the useful by-products of meetings in a more focused and effective way.

Change needs to stretch but not
break your corporate culture

A lack of coherence with your corporate culture can doom change projects to failure. If you want to make a major and sustained change in ways of working you need to find ways to make the change successful within the values of your corporate culture.

The alternative of breaking and fundamentally changing your corporate culture is only really open to you during major crises or, more slowly, with a great deal of support from the top.

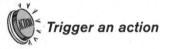 *Trigger an action*

Schedule a discussion with your colleagues.

What are the corporate cultural beliefs and practices that cause you to meet too often in your business?

How can you position your initiative as consistent with what the culture values?

How can you get the useful by-products without having too many meetings?

PART 2

Save a day a week by killing unnecessary meetings and topics and removing unnecessary participants

. . .

In Part 2 we will take some simple steps to kill unnecessary meetings and topics and cut out unnecessary participants.

Implementing this part of the book first will give you most of the savings outlined in your business case – up to a day per week per person of unnecessary meeting attendance.

Only once we have done this will we move on in Parts 3 and 4 to improve the design and running of the remaining meetings that do need to happen.

Our research and observation of meetings in many leading organizations shows that:

- 50 percent of meeting content is not relevant to participants or does not need to be discussed collectively
- Up to 20 percent of participants should not be there

If you have completed the business case from Chapter 1 already, you will have your own organization's numbers and can see that this is a massive opportunity to reduce cost and improve people's working lives by cutting out work that does not need doing.

This is a tremendous win-win and needs almost no investment on your part to implement. However, turning down meetings, refusing topics, and asking people not to attend your meetings can be countercultural and can lead to sensitive discussions – even though those are probably with the same people who complain about poor quality meetings as well.

The next three chapters will give you some tools and concepts for doing this. It is important to frame this as being about effectiveness and engagement and to make what you are doing congruent with your corporate culture.

This is not about refusing to collaborate, it is about collaborating more effectively, delivering your outcomes faster, and freeing people from unnecessary work.

We suggest you focus these improvement efforts on your own meetings and on the top 10–15 percent of managers and professionals in your organization.

....

- **Chapter 3** – Saying no to more meetings
- **Chapter 4** – Killing unnecessary topics
- **Chapter 5** – Removing unnecessary participants

Chapter 3

Saying no to more meetings

....

 Actions – turn down at least two meeting invites in the next week where there is not a clear agenda or value in you attending

 Target – save yourself at least a day of meetings in the next month

....

Step one in reducing the number of face-to-face and virtual meetings you attend lies in changing the way you respond to meeting invitations. If you systematically refuse to add any more poor quality meetings to your schedule, then your number of unnecessary meetings will inevitably decline over time.

Later chapters will show you how to disengage from the unnecessary topics and meetings that you already attend.

Your time is your most important resource; protect it and do not allow others to fill it with unnecessary meetings, calls, and webinars – be deliberate about how you allocate your time.

Three good reasons to attend a meeting

There are of course many good reasons to attend meetings. You should normally accept invitations to meetings where:

Your expertise needs to be shared with the group to make a decision or conclude some collaborative work	✓
The topic requires live "synchronous" (same time) interaction between yourself and others to succeed	✓
You need to build relationships, or deal with sensitive issues such as negotiation, or conflict resolution with others	✓

Six top reasons for declining

However, many meetings are a waste of time. You should consider rejecting meetings where:

There is no clear outcome from the meeting or topic specified in advance	✗
The wrong people are attending	✗
The meeting will discuss matters of low relevance to you	✗
You have no role except to listen	✗
The meeting objectives would be better delivered in one-to-one discussions, or in smaller sub-teams	✗
You could meet the objective of the meeting through email	✗

We will look at how to deal with these common problems in your meetings in detail in later chapters; at this stage just use them as criteria for considering whether you should attend new meetings you are invited to or not.

Take some time to reflect on the meetings you already attend. Think about the parts that are most relevant and the parts that are least relevant. What kind of topics do you want and need to be involved in, and which do not have sufficient value to be worth your time?

Which meetings you attend and topics in those meetings are a good use of your time?	
Which meetings and topics are not relevant and are a waste of your time?	

By saying no to future unnecessary meetings, you can "stop the rot" and make sure the problem doesn't get any worse; we will then move on to disconnect ourselves from the unnecessary meetings and topics we already attend.

Here are some ideas you might find useful in saying no.

Pushing back gracefully

If you receive an invite to a meeting, do not automatically accept. Ask for more details, particularly if there is no clear agenda or outcome.

If you use Outlook as your diary you can reply as "Tentative" rather than "Accept" and ask a couple of questions.

This can range from the very direct: "Thanks for your invitation. Can you let me know what the outcomes of the meeting will be and specifically where I can add value so I can see how I can help and prepare properly?" to the more pointed: "I am very busy at the moment and trying to prioritize my time. Could you send me an agenda letting me know the specific input you need from me and whether there is another way I can provide that without attending the meeting?"

It is often easier, particularly if you think this is a sensitive issue, to pick up the phone and have a short conversation with the meeting leader.

The right style will depend on your personal preferences, your position, and your corporate culture. If you are a less senior attendee, you may find it difficult to challenge an established meetings culture and expectation of attending; we hope that this book will give you a language and methodology for at least having this conversation with your boss or meetings chairman. Why not get them a copy of this book?

The important thing is to challenge the assumption that you will attend every meeting mindlessly.

"In our organization if an agenda for a regular meeting has not been circulated seven days before the meeting, it is automatically canceled."
                    Project manager, technology company, Germany

For existing meetings, if you have not received an agenda a few days before, pick up the phone or send an email to see if the meeting is still on and if you are still needed.

Just putting this initial barrier in the way throws up some

opportunities to provide input without attending a meeting. For example:

- Can you brief someone else who is attending the meeting?
- If there are multiple people attending from your department, could one attend and inform the others later?
- Can you meet the needs of the meeting organizer without attending? (This is a win-win.)

If people do not respond to your request for clarity on the agenda, this tells you that the meeting will probably be badly organized and you should not really attend. If you choose to attend, you are deciding that your time is less valuable than whatever others choose to fill it with.

The meeting organizer may well have a good reason for you to attend, but if they do not you should have a conversation to find out whether it is worth your while to be there.

Some specific questions to ask include:

- What input exactly do you need from me at the meeting?
- Is there any way I can give you that outside the meeting? Such as by getting a copy of the minutes afterwards or having a one-to-one conversation beforehand
- Which specific topics require my attendance? Is it OK if I just attend for these parts?
- For face-to-face meetings requiring travel, ask if you can join just for your topic by video or web conference

If you can't get good answers to these questions and the meeting organizer still wants you to attend, it becomes a judgment call.

In some corporate cultures, it can be hard to say no; in others, you are expected to.

Remember to frame your reason for not attending the meeting as something that is valued in your culture. If your culture values customers, then you are trying to free up more time to get in front of and serve customers. If your culture values efficiency, then make the efficiency argument. If you do not give context by explaining what you are doing, people may simply see you as uncooperative.

You will probably find that just putting these barriers in the way of easy acceptance will enable you to meet your target of turning down two or more meetings in the first week. If you do this systematically, over time you will eventually eliminate most unnecessary meetings.

Dave Grady in his TED talk "How to Save the World or at Least Yourself from Bad Meetings," calls accepting too many meeting invites MAS – "mindless acceptance syndrome." He notes that you would not allow people to walk up to your desk and steal your chair without a good reason but we regularly allow people to steal our time without good reason.

If you do not feel confident implementing this first step yourself then schedule some time with your manager, explain your problem with meeting overload, and discuss how you can disengage from some of your meetings.

Make the cost explicit

Meetings can often seem as if they are "free." After all, we are already paying people's salaries and the meeting rooms may be just down the hall. However, meetings always have a cost in terms of time and lost opportunity.

At Global Integration, we have people based around the world so our face-to-face meetings with travel, venues, and time away from client work can cost $100,000 each, and as a result we think carefully about when we meet.

If you are being asked to travel to a meeting or to give up a significant amount of time, then make the cost explicit.

"My boss asked me to travel from the UK to the west coast of the US for a meeting. I pointed out that this would take three days of my time and over $7,000 in expenses and asked if my attendance was worth that, or whether I could join the call for an hour by telephone? My boss quickly agreed."

Marketing manager, tech industry, UK

Alternatively, you can make this about the opportunity cost of attending: is this more important than completing the other urgent work you have committed to deliver?

Some of our participants use live meeting calculators, which are freely available as smartphone apps. You select the number of people attending a meeting and their average salary and the app displays a live running total of the cost of the meeting as it continues. This is a great way to keep people focused on the cost of the meeting.

"If our boss gets concerned with how long the meeting is taking, he opens the app and lets us know how much this discussion is costing – it is amazing how fast we then find we can conclude the discussion."

Financial services manager, Hong Kong

"At our big events and conferences, we start with a slide show-
ing how much more product we will need to sell to cover the
cost of running this event – the events are then focused on
delivering at least this level of improved productivity."

Technical quality manager, consumer goods, USA

Your time is your most valuable resource; if people think it is
free they will often abuse it. By putting a cost on our time, we
make the value explicit.

Open a personal meeting bank account

Consider setting yourself a meetings budget or bank account. Make
an explicit decision about how much of your week you can afford
to spend in meetings given all the other work you need to complete.

When you reach this limit, only accept a new meeting if you
cancel an existing one. This way you never go "overdrawn" in
the time you want to allocate.

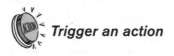 *Trigger an action*

Put a reminder on a Post-it note on your desk or on your diary
to challenge new meeting invites you receive.

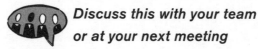 *Discuss this with your team*
or at your next meeting

• Set the expectation that it is OK to decline or question
  meetings

- Model it yourself; ask "Is there anyone here who is not sure that this meeting is a good use of their time?" If so, consider if they should attend in future
- Send out a meeting evaluation asking how the meeting could be improved to make it a better use of participants' time
- Respond positively to people who ask for more information about your meetings
- Ask your meeting participants to read this book too

Chapter 4

Killing unnecessary topics

Actions – identify and remove topics that should not be discussed collectively in your meetings

Target – cut 20 percent of the length of your meetings by killing unnecessary topics

In Chapter 3, "Saying no to more meetings," you started to push back against your new meeting invites.

In this chapter, we will analyze our existing face-to-face, conference call, video, and web meetings to find unnecessary topics and meetings.

Unnecessary topics

In our work with thousands of meetings around the world, we have learned that many topics that are included in traditional meetings should not even be on the agenda.

- We share information that is not relevant to many attendees or that the individuals in the meeting cannot use to do
  anything differently
- We use meetings when other methods such as email or
  one-to-one conversations would be much more effective
- We design meetings that do not need participation from
  the attendees
- We are not clear about the outcomes we want from
  discussing many topics

This is a huge and frustrating waste of time. In this chapter, you
will learn how to analyze where your meetings are making some
of the classic meeting mistakes and generate ideas on what to do
about them.

Finding and dealing with unnecessary meeting topics

Use the meetings tick chart below to analyze the meetings, calls,
video, or webinars that you run, or that consume a lot of your
time.

Based on this information, you will be able to apply the guidelines later in this book to cut out unnecessary meeting topics
and even kill whole meetings.

HOW TO USE THIS TICK CHART

Create a simple spreadsheet or chart like the one below. List the
topics or agenda items of your meeting in the left-hand column,
and the names of the participants in the rows across the top.

Here is an example from a meeting we observed.

TOPICS ↓	PARTICIPANTS BOSS H	TL	JM	SS	FG	BM	BK
1. BUSINESS UPDATES	✓✓		✓				
2. STATUS REPORTS	✓✓✓✓✓✓	✓	✓	✓	✓	✓	
3. MARKETING UPDATE	✓✓✓	✓✓✓	✓✓✓				
4. NEXT YEAR'S PLAN	✓✓✓✓✓	✓✓✓✓✓	✓✓✓	✓✓✓	✓✓✓✓✓	✓✓✓✓✓	
5. BUDGETS	✓✓✓✓			✓✓✓✓			
6. PEOPLE & TALENT	✓✓✓✓	✓✓✓✓✓	✓✓✓✓✓	✓✓✓✓	✓✓✓	✓✓✓✓	
7. SUPPLY CHAIN ISSUES							✓

During your meeting, when any individual talks during the discussion of each of the topics, make a tick under their name (two ticks if they talk for a long time).

This will give you a graphical record of who contributed to each of the topics and will help you identify which topics were relevant to which attendees.

Frequency of talking is, of course, not the only indicator of participation and relevance but it is easy to identify and enables you to initiate a conversation based around some facts and patterns after the meeting.

It is also an important indicator of the collective value of an individual attending the meeting. If they do not contribute they may learn from others, but the others won't learn from them. If the information flow is all one way, as we will see below, then a meeting may not be the right way to involve them.

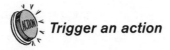 **Trigger an action**

Make a note in your diary now to take a copy of the meetings tick chart to your next meeting and record every time someone speaks.

Interpreting the results

In our client work, when we sit in and observe live meetings, we have found that around 40 percent of meeting content is not relevant to all attendees.

By cutting out low-relevance topics from our meetings we can improve the effectiveness of what remains and set up more focused sub-team meetings or one-to-one conversations to deal with important issues that are best handled outside the meeting.

There are two main types of interactions in meetings:

1. Star group interactions – these tend to be either

- One-to-one conversations, which are often of low relevance to everyone else or
- Broadcasts of information from one individual (often the boss or an expert) to the group

We call these types of communication "star group" (hub and spoke) interactions.

Because they are individual or broadcast conversations, they do not really require a collective meeting where everyone needs to attend synchronously (at the same time, if not the same place).

Typical examples of star group interactions include:

- Broadcasting information from one person (usually the boss) to many without any opportunity to interact or do anything with the information. Topic 1, the business updates in our meeting tick chart above, was one of these, where the boss gave an update and only one person asked a question. This information could have been circulated in advance as there was little need for discussion

- Status updates, where people describe what they did last week but the information is only relevant to them and their boss. You can see this in our meeting tick chart example above in topic 2, "status reports": everyone spoke just to give their update; the boss asked a few questions but no one else asked questions of each other. While this can be a good use of the boss's time, the other participants spend a lot of time listening to information that is not relevant to them

- Individual action reviews, where people update their boss or the meeting leader on individual activities or deliverables such as project updates that are not relevant to other participants. We could achieve the same objective with a series of one-to-one calls, saving significant time for the other participants

- Detailed discussions that are relevant to the meeting leader or presenter and one other person but not relevant or interesting to others. Topic 5, "budgets" on our tick chart example above, was one of these

- Side discussions or digressions between individuals that are not relevant to the topic being covered

On your meetings tick chart make a note where any topics mainly or wholly consist of **one-to-one interaction or broadcast content**.

As you make a tick after every person talks you will quickly spot these star group topics – you will see that only one person talks or only a couple of people contribute in each conversation.

If this is your own meeting, be particularly aware of the interactions of others. If you are the central "hub" person in a star group, you may feel that all the topics are relevant – because they are to you personally. You should also ask yourself whether the topics are relevant to all other participants as well.

Early in Alan's career he attended a weekly sales meeting with five-minute status updates from each member of a team of 12 people. When he questioned the value of the meeting he found that the manager was only doing it because they thought it was what the team wanted, and the team members were only doing it because they thought the team leader insisted on it. Nobody found it useful and the team decided to stop doing it.

This was a simple meeting that lasted about 60 minutes with about 15 minutes of preparation. Even so, this one meeting consumed an hour per week of sales time for 13 people, the equivalent of wasting one-third of a salesperson, or over 600 hours every year with no real benefits.

2. "Spaghetti" interaction

We call work that requires synchronous communication, discussion, co-creation, and active participation "spaghetti" because people must work in a highly interconnected way to achieve a collaborative goal.

Typical examples of spaghetti team interactions include:

- Discussions to make a decision
- Multidisciplinary problem-solving
- Co-creating new ideas and proposals live in the meeting
- Solving common problems
- Learning common skills

On our meetings tick chart topics 4, "next year's plan," and 6, "people and talent," look like spaghetti topics, where everyone was engaged and contributing.

Some spaghetti interaction, however, is only relevant to a **subset** of the people at the meeting. It is quite common that meetings can have several topics that are only relevant to a few people who attend.

You can see this pattern on our meetings tick chart above for topic 3, "marketing update," which was very relevant to three people who spoke a lot, but most people did not contribute at all.

If some topics in your meeting are only relevant to a subset of meeting attendees, then these topics should be discussed at smaller sub-team meetings attended only by the people who need to be involved.

If the topics are **relevant and create interaction from all participants**, then these are the kind of topics we should base our future collective meetings around.

If topics are not relevant to all, there are usually other, simpler ways to deliver the objective.

Redesign your meeting based on these patterns
....

Review the information on your meetings tick chart by looking at the pattern of ticks horizontally for each of the topics.

You can now redesign your meeting based on this information.

1. Where topics were mainly one-to-one conversations or broadcasts of information

These are of low relevance to most participants and can be handled without a meeting.

- **One-to-ones**: these should be handled outside the meeting by the individuals concerned. Allowing individual side conversations can waste a lot of the other participants' time. These topics are where only two people interacted on your meetings tick chart
- **Broadcasts**: the one-way transmission and passive consumption of information and presentations do not require people to be in the same place at the same time. These are topics where the person making the broadcast talked a lot but the other participants did not interact much or at all.

    Because a lot of information-giving does not require synchronous communication, asynchronous tools, such as email, blogs, or file sharing are much more cost- and time-effective, particularly for teams that operate across multiple locations and time zones.

    If the "broadcast" information is essential to the later conduct of the meeting, for example sharing information on which a decision or discussion will be based, then this information should normally be sent out in advance for pre-reading. See Chapter 9 for more tips on taking information-giving out of your meeting

"I cut out status reports and personal updates. Nobody seemed to miss them and we used some of the time saved to talk about things that were much more relevant and important."
Brand team manager, pharmaceuticals, France

In Chapter 1 we referred to a study of an executive committee meeting that consumed 300,000 hours of time per year, at a cost of around $15 million per year. The stated objective of this executive committee meeting was "to provide **updates** on all phases of the business."

We do not have personal knowledge of this meeting, but that objective is likely to lead to a lot of classic star group content — updates and status reviews. Most of that meeting objective could be met through email or shared files. Is it worth 300,000 hours and $15 million every year? Is this how an executive committee should be spending its time?

2. Where topics were relevant to some, but not all, participants

Some topics generate interaction from several participants, but not all. They are useful topics to discuss, but not for everybody. We can waste time informing people who do not need to know about the agenda item and having to engage people who are not really involved can reduce the quality and speed of decision-making.

If you are the meeting leader you should set up separate meetings to discuss these topics with a more limited set of participants for whom these topics are directly relevant.

You can also place topics relevant to everyone at the beginning of the meeting, and then allow some people to leave so that the remaining participants can focus on issues that are only relevant to them.

3. Where topics were relevant to everybody attending

If you have topics where every individual interacted, congratulations; these are the topics that form the basis of a great meeting. Meetings should ideally be based **only** around topics that are relevant to all participants.

However, just because the topic is relevant and creates interaction, this does not necessarily mean that it requires a face-to-face meeting to deal with it. It is always worth asking:

- Is a meeting the best way to deal with this topic?
- Could it be handled by an empowered individual or sub-team instead?
- Could we use technology to replace a face-to-face meeting, or reduce our travel?

Pattern	Diagnosis	Action
Only 2 individuals engaged	One to one – star group	Take outside the meeting
One person talks, little interaction from others	Broadcast – star group	Send information before the meeting
A small number of people very engaged, others not	Relevant to some but not all – spaghetti sub-team	Hold sub-meetings with only the relevant people
Everyone engaged	Spaghetti topics	Check these really need a live meeting then use these as your core agenda

Going back to our 300,000-hour, $15 million per year executive committee, instead of sharing updates, what topics are likely to be relevant to every member of an executive committee?

Topics we have found to constitute executive team "spaghetti," where everyone is engaged include:

- Strategy development
- Succession and people planning
- Common learning
- Community and relationship building
- Evaluation of high potentials
- Communication strategy

Executive teams also typically contain several sub-teams discussing specific issues that are relevant to a few members but not everyone.

IF YOU DO NOT NEED PARTICIPATION FROM THE ATTENDEES, YOU DO NOT NEED A MEETING

If all you need to do is transmit information for common understanding, you can do that through technology. If certain topics seem relevant, but have low levels of participation, then you can probably redesign them to improve your meetings. We will look at how to do this in later chapters.

Ask yourself: "Was the outcome worthwhile? Was what we got out of discussing the topic worth the cost and effort we put into it?"

If your remaining meeting topics pass these challenges, then **focus your future meetings on these topics** and make sure you allow time for them to be resolved fully.

Please keep a copy of your meetings tick chart as we will refer to it in future chapters.

If you are not a meeting leader and do not have the power to implement these changes yourself, why not show this approach to the leader and suggest you do the analysis at your next meeting? Then sit down and interpret the results and recommendations together afterwards.

If you engage meeting participants in deciding together what is most relevant to them and in redesigning meetings that make better use of their time, you normally get a very positive response.

If none of the topics at a regular meeting pass the "spaghetti" test, then maybe you do not need that meeting at all.

Example: The management meeting
Management meetings often suffer from too much information-sharing. Whether this is the executive committee of the whole business or a management team for a business unit or other operation, management teams tend to think they need to know what is going on in detail in their business.

Unfortunately, when they focus on this level of detail, they often do not have the time left to discuss the important and truly collaborative outcomes they need to drive the business forward.

We worked with the management team of a European business in the telecoms sector. They had a monthly management meeting which consisted mainly of functional and geographic reviews. The heads of the countries reviewed their operations in detail. Each country and function spent about 45 minutes telling their colleagues what they had been doing and what the issues were.

There was relatively little discussion unless it involved a subset of the members, for example the country manager, finance, and manufacturing directors discussing what was happening in a particular country.

When we observed the meeting, we did not identify a single topic where all team members were engaged and involved.

Despite their monthly meetings, the management team found it difficult to get enough time to discuss truly collaborative issues like succession or strategy.

This was a classic star group meeting with individuals sharing information that was not relevant to all other individuals. If you are the HR director in this meeting, listening to a country review, you are only listening to see if there is anything there with implications for HR.

If you are another country manager you are listening to see if there's anything that might be relevant to your country. There is the potential for relevance, but sharing a lot of information is an inefficient process for doing it.

After discussing the meeting with the participants, we helped them re-engineer the meeting around increased relevance.

They replaced the country and functional reviews with a much shorter update process. The management team members wanted to know what was going on at a high level across the business and to ask questions; however they all agreed they did not need as much detail as they had in the past.

In the new process, each head had just three slides which they had to complete in seven minutes or less:

- *The first slide showed their overall business performance on agreed metrics. This slide was in the same format every time so they did not need to keep explaining what people were looking at. The presenter only needed to explain any measures that were "red" (underperforming)*

- *The second slide showed anything that was happening in their area that had implications for other people around the table – focused and directly relevant information for other attendees*
- *The third slide was to share anything that the presenter was proud of or thought was great – we all need an opportunity to do this*

For the eight members of the team, a process that used to take all day now took about an hour.

The rest of the half-day meeting concentrated on truly collaborative (spaghetti team) issues where the management team members needed to work together to create a common output. This was based around a calendar for strategy development, succession planning, and other common issues. For the first time, they had time to really debate and resolve these important issues.

The members of the team felt that, as leaders of the business, they needed to have a better understanding of what was happening in their different locations and functions. However, they weren't really getting this information from the functional and geographic updates in the previous agenda.

In the new design, the afternoon of the monthly meeting was spent visiting a location or function, talking to the people and seeing in more detail some of the important projects that were being developed there.

In the first meeting the management team spent some time working in a factory and understanding the new quality process. The second meeting was held at one of the country offices where they could meet different people and join customer visits.

The management meeting members felt these meetings were a much better use of their time, gave a much better understanding of the business and enabled them to address some critical collaborative outcomes they had struggled to deliver in the past.

The critical steps in redesigning this meeting were:

- Identifying the real spaghetti for this team – what their unique collaborative outcomes were as a team
- Systematizing the information-giving and star group parts of the meeting to improve relevance and shorten the time allocated
- Designing the new agenda for participation, action, and engagement

Management meetings regularly consume a day per month or 5 percent of your most senior leaders' time and attention. As we've seen in previous chapters, they also generate a huge amount of additional preparation time.

These meetings set the tone for the meetings below them. If we can find demonstrably better ways to run management meetings, then the attendees will want to apply them to their own meetings and the process will cascade down the organization.

In making a change in scale in the way you meet across the organization, you want these ideas to be aspirational. If you can demonstrate the value and persuade your senior leaders to become evangelists for the change, this is much easier.

Example: The team meeting
The key challenge for team meetings is to keep the focus on the collective outcomes of the team.

Many people seem to think that just because it is on the agenda of the team meeting, it is automatically a team issue. As with any meeting, the secret is to focus on the spaghetti.

Team meetings run relatively regularly in many organizations and their planning can become an afterthought or based around the same topics every time. It is tempting for individuals at a team meeting to just share what they have been doing or to present the outputs of the major piece of work that is being done by members of the team.

Often "push style" star group content can make up a lot of the agenda with team members being informed of business results and the latest corporate initiatives with little opportunity to participate.

We helped re-engineer an IT team meeting from a series of activity updates and status reviews to something much more focused on the spaghetti. The team identified the following outcomes as being relevant to all team members:
* *Building the networks and relationships of the team: the team operated virtually for most of the time and needed strong relationships to make collaboration easy during the virtual working phases*

- *Implementing common learning to improve the performance of the team: because the team members were the individual representatives of the function in their different locations, they did not get much chance to learn from their local colleagues. They needed to share best practice and learn new things together*
- *Resolving business issues or conflicts between individuals and small groups that were difficult to resolve virtually. This was not full team spaghetti as not everyone was involved, but most people needed to have those small group conversations at some point during the meeting*
- *The manager wanted to give a business update: he realized this was a classic star group task but felt it was important and wanted to find a way to make it more interactive*

We helped them redesign their meeting to include:
- *Sending out the business update in advance and running a quiz for participants at the beginning of the meeting*
- *Focusing on outcomes that require the participation of all team members*
- *Running a "wants and offers" best practice sharing session which focused on identifying topics where people had a specific need (a want) in advance and then identifying the people who could help with this (an offer) and putting them together for short discussions*
- *More structured community time to ensure mixing of the participants and social time together in the evenings in small but changing conversational groups*

- *Allowing unstructured time in the agenda for two- and three-person mini-discussions to happen*
- *A short training session on new ideas or techniques for the team*
- *A rotating meeting owner so that each meeting has a slightly different style and to share the workload*

It is important to engage the members of a team in the redesign of their meetings so that they have a sense of ownership. Given that they will regularly attend these meetings, it is in their interests to find a design that is relevant and engaging.

The know, feel, or do test

A useful test of meeting quality is to ask participants what they know, feel, or do differently because of discussing the topic or attending the meeting.

If they have not taken away any actions or any knowledge that will help them do their job or improve their motivation to perform, then you should question whether the topics were worth the time of that audience.

POINT TO THE SPAGHETTI

"We liked the star and spaghetti language so we bought plates of plastic spaghetti and plastic starfish and use them in our meetings. If topics are straying into star group territory someone will point to one of the plates or ask the question, 'Is this really spaghetti?' Often this is enough to stop digressions or wasting time on issues only relevant to a small number of people."

Finance manager, packaged goods, Brazil

While you are embedding the techniques, it can be useful to get participants to give feedback after every topic. Give people a piece of paper with a picture of spaghetti on one side and a picture of a star on the other; after the topic ask them to hold up the side of the paper showing whether they thought the topic you just discussed was spaghetti or star.

If people have different perceptions of what is star and what is spaghetti this is an extremely useful discussion to have and may determine how you run your future meetings.

Working in a regulated world

If you work in a highly regulated or controlled industry or organization you may find some of your meetings are full of unnecessary topics by our definitions, but you have no choice but to comply with them for legal reasons.

For example, some financial services organizations are now compelled to hold regular review meetings where individuals have a legal responsibility to attend, review, and share information. In regulated industries like pharmaceuticals you may need to demonstrate to a regulator that you have attended certain meetings and approved information on certain topics.

These meetings are often designed by regulators or lawyers whose objectives are very different from those of us trying to run efficient and engaging meetings. The meetings are often based on a lack of trust of participants or to mitigate risks that regulators think are unacceptable.

Even if you are not in a regulated industry, you may have some internal governance and control meetings that are designed around these principles.

You may have no choice but to attend these mandatory meetings. However, it is important to stop this mindset leaking out into all your other meetings. Not all meetings, even in highly regulated or controlled organizations, need to be held this way and you should still have significant opportunities to implement these ideas outside your core governance meetings.

Meetings are an important carrier of control in organizations, so the principles in this book can help you push back where this level of control is unnecessary.

More resources

You can find out more about the idea of "star groups" and "spaghetti team working" in our book *Speed Lead: Faster, Simpler Ways to Manage People, Projects and Teams in Complex Companies.*

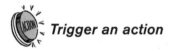 **Trigger an action**

Many people read business books, nod along with the content but do not act to change anything. Take out your diary right now, find your next big meeting and put a note in your diary the day before to prepare a meetings tick chart for the meeting.

If you do this, the reminder to act will pop up just at the time you need it and you'll be much more likely to implement the idea.

Now schedule some time afterwards with the meeting leader to discuss what you found.

If you really want to save yourself a day a week or more, you need to take some actions. If you do not, you will still be attending unnecessary meetings in your retirement year.

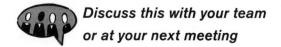 **Discuss this with your team or at your next meeting**

If your meeting is a regular one, encourage the other people at your meeting to read this book so they can see what you are trying to achieve and understand the methodology.

Share the results of your analysis of the meeting interactions and drive a discussion on:

- Where is the spaghetti? What are the topics that are relevant and engaging for all participants and need to be discussed live in our meeting? These should form the core agenda for future meetings
- Where do we need sub-meetings? What topics are only relevant for a subset of the attendees and only need a limited audience? How will we handle these?
- What topics are "star" and only require one-to-one or broadcast communication? How can we organize these so we do not have to cover them in our meeting?
- From this discussion develop a core agenda for future meetings based on the key "spaghetti" topics that you need everyone to be engaged in

Chapter 5

Removing unnecessary participants

 Actions – identify the unnecessary participants at your meeting and challenge their attendance

 Target – reduce the number of people at your meeting by at least one or 10 percent, whichever is greater

In the last chapter we focused on eliminating unnecessary topics from our meetings. Next, we will consider whether some **participants** do not need to attend our meeting.

Having unnecessary participants is an additional cost and makes it more difficult to achieve alignment and clarity and to make decisions.

We need to spend time educating and involving people and considering their views. If they do not bring anything to the meeting or decision, or are not important to implementation, then this can be a waste of everyone's time in the meeting.

It is also a waste of their time; the unnecessary participants should be and usually are delighted to escape. Unfortunately, however, a small number of individuals react badly to being excluded as they think this reflects on their status and this can lead to a difficult, if necessary, conversation.

Internal surveys and data from observing meetings in our clients suggest that 10–20 percent of participants at meetings **should not be attending at all.**

On conference calls and webinars these participants probably dial in and then disappear or "multitask"; at least in virtual meetings they do not have to sit there and try to look interested!

In this chapter, we will show you how to identify unnecessary participants by:

• Analyzing their interactions in meetings
• Recognizing and dealing with some typical unhelpful participant types
• Using some simple tools to discuss who really needs to attend your meetings, and who does not

Analyze meeting participation, worked example

You have probably already captured some useful information to identify unnecessary participants from your meetings tick chart in Chapter 4.

Look back at this information or, if you have not done this yet, go back and use the meetings tick chart to analyze participant activity at your meetings. You should kill unnecessary topics first; it can be difficult to identify who really needs to attend without doing this first.

In the meetings tick chart exercise, you made a tick under a participant's name every time they spoke in each of the topics.

You have already used the patterns of participation on the sheet to help identify where **topics** are relevant to everyone, a subset or just individuals. We did this by looking at patterns of interaction **horizontally** across the columns.

Now use the same information and look at the **vertical** participant columns.

TOPICS ↓	PARTICIPANTS BOSS H	TL	JM	SS	FG	BM	BK
1. BUSINESS UPDATES	✓✓		✓				
2. STATUS REPORTS	✓✓✓✓✓	✓	✓	✓	✓	✓	
3. MARKETING UPDATE	✓✓✓	✓✓✓	✓✓✓				
4. NEXT YEAR'S PLAN	✓✓✓✓	✓✓✓✓	✓✓✓	✓✓✓	✓✓✓✓	✓✓✓✓	
5. BUDGETS	✓✓✓✓			✓✓✓✓✓			
6. PEOPLE & TALENT	✓✓✓✓	✓✓✓✓	✓✓✓✓	✓✓✓	✓✓✓	✓✓✓	
7. SUPPLY CHAIN ISSUES							✓

If a participant has very low levels of engagement and participation, then ask why they attend the meeting or the specific topic.

The number of occasions someone speaks is not the only measure of participation. Some people think more deeply and rarely contribute explicitly, but when they do they bring great value. Others are probably sitting there wondering why they were invited.

It is also true that people who speak constantly are not necessarily good participants. If people talk a lot, but add no value, you should also challenge their participation.

There are also some cultural differences in how people participate around the world. If you are working with an international group of participants, please read Chapter 10.

In either case, it is worthwhile having a conversation with these individuals about the value of their attendance to both themselves and the meeting. For example, if people are only attending to stay informed, you may be able to meet their needs much more efficiently by sending them the actions after the meeting. If there are people you need to consult or get input from on specific topics, then consider consulting them one-to-one before the meeting.

In the tick chart example above we asked the individual in the last column (BK) why they attended this regular marketing meeting.

"Two years previously there was a supply chain issue that had not been communicated to marketing. Marketing suggested that someone from supply chain attend the meetings in future to make sure this did not happen again.

I only speak to give the supply chain update which is usually "no current problems." Nobody asks any questions unless there is a problem and I don't feel able to contribute to any of the other topics at all."

Supply chain manager, packaged goods, Belgium

We discussed this and quickly agreed that he could check in with the marketing meeting chairperson just before each meeting and let them know if there were any problems. If more detail was required, he would join by video conference for 30 minutes.

BK was delighted: it saved him attending four global meetings per year.

In our experience, working with meetings around the world, people are often relieved to be given "permission" not to attend irrelevant meetings, so there is a real "win-win" here.

You already know who they are

"When we were asked to identify one unnecessary person from our meeting it was not difficult – everyone, including the individual concerned, identified the same person. She was pleased she could get out of coming in future."

HR manager, business services, India

In our experience, when we state that 10 percent or more of meeting participants are unnecessary, most people look at each other and admit that they already know who these individuals are.

If you had to remove one person from your regular meeting, who would it be? If you already know the answer, they probably do too.

At this point in our writing we had a lively disagreement. Kevan's approach as a CEO and consultant was to let people know directly that they were not necessary to the meeting. Alan maintained that this is hard to do with your peers or people who may be senior to you. It is important to find a more indirect and polite way of raising the issue if you feel it is appropriate.

A lot of people feel uncomfortable in challenging attendance at meetings. We developed the meetings tick chart to give you some objective data to initiate a discussion. You can position the discussion as "I noticed that you did not feel the need to participate a lot in these topics or this meeting; what would make this a better meeting for you, or do you think it is really a good use of your time?" and talk them through the data.

The important thing is that you or the meeting leader initiate a conversation. You will probably find that the individuals concerned are relieved to get out of the meeting.

Challenge unhelpful participants

There are usually three main types of problem participants at meetings:

Those who do not need to be there

These participants may attend for historic reasons (they used to be involved but the meeting has moved on) or for other goals that do not help the conduct of the meeting.

For example, we all know individuals who seem to go to meetings to improve their "visibility," even though they may have little to add to the discussion. They keep bringing the conversation around to what they have been doing or other things that make them look good, even if they aren't relevant or helpful to the topics being discussed.

There are more effective ways to be visible and build your network than sitting in irrelevant meetings where you add no value. However, if this is the only mechanism that exists in your company for being visible, it may be rational to attend from that individual's perspective.

Talk to these individuals to see what value they think they bring to the meeting and what specific actions they take away. If they can't explain this clearly, challenge whether they need to attend in future.

Those who do need to attend but only for part of the time

These are participants who need to attend for some specific topics, but not for everything. We need to organize our meetings so these people can only attend for their section and be confident enough to say when the meeting is no longer relevant for them so they can get back to work.

Be explicit in your meetings that you accept and expect people to leave after they have attended the relevant parts of the meeting. Make a point of thanking and praising people who do this.

Those who you do need to attend but are not present

There are some participants who are important but either do not attend, send deputies, or do not pay attention when they are present. In each case, we need to find a way to get them to attend fully.

- **Stand-ins**: these are people who regularly do not attend or who send deputies or stand-ins to your meeting; this usually means that your meeting is not important to them.

  Your first step should be to think about whether they are relevant to your meeting and whether your meeting is relevant to them. Also, make sure your meeting is well organized as people will always find reasons not to attend badly run meetings.

If these people are not necessary to the success of the meeting, then their stand-ins do not need to attend either. If they are critical, then you need to get the right people in the room.

Schedule a discussion with these people to identify who is the right person to attend to make your meeting a success. Be prepared to reject stand-ins if this is important

- **Multitaskers**: question people who constantly multitask in the meeting. It may be that they are right and the latest email or text is genuinely more relevant and important to them than the content of the meeting. If so, they should focus on their priorities and step out of the room so as not to distract the others. This makes it possible to deal with urgent matters but prevents trivial interruptions.

  If you do need this individual to be fully focused on the meeting, then you need to discuss with them how they can control their multitasking in your meeting. This may require more regular breaks, switching off phones, etc.

  Designing for higher levels of engagement and participation will also limit the tendency to be distracted.

  Having the right participants there for each meeting topic is critical. If an important participant is missing you should consider cancelling the meeting, otherwise you will just have to repeat it when they are available.

Type of unhelpful participant	Action
Those who do not need to be there at all	Challenge their attendance
Those who do need to attend but only for part of the time	Encourage them to attend only for their topic
Stand-ins	Evaluate who really needs to attend and discuss getting the right person there
Multitaskers	Discuss how to keep their attention, increase participation or ask them to step outside to deal with the other task

The bus check

In his book, *Good to Great*, Jim Collins writes about "getting the right people on the bus." Some of our clients apply this idea to meetings.

From time to time the meeting leader or facilitator does a "bus check" by asking the question: "Who needs to be on this bus (meeting) for the next stage of the journey?"

This is an explicit check that the same participants who currently attend your regular meetings still need to be involved in the future. This is a great way of continually refining your meeting membership and gives you a regular excuse to challenge participation and relevance.

You may need to remove some existing members or invite some new people if the nature or the phase of the activity has changed.

"I asked two people who sat on our global project meetings if they really needed to attend the meetings for the next phase of the project. Both were relieved; they had been coming mainly

because they thought I wanted them to! It saved all of us time and money."

Project head, distribution, UK

Why not run a bus check discussion at your next meeting?

Define core or on-demand meeting members

It can be very helpful to separate participants into a core group who attend all parts of the meeting and an "on-demand" extended group who are invited to attend only if there is a specific topic or expertise required. The membership of these groups will depend on the objectives and outcomes you require from the meeting and the topics within it.

• Who are your core and on-demand members?
• When should on-demand members attend?

If you are not the meeting leader or do not have the confidence or power to challenge the attendance of unnecessary participants, why not schedule a meeting with your manager or meeting leader to share your concerns?

What if the unnecessary participant is you?

In Chapter 3, "Saying no to more meetings," we introduced a process for challenging your attendance at new meetings. Take the time now to think about your attendance at the regular meetings you participate in. Are you engaged, do you participate in the meeting, is it a good use of your time?

If you are an unnecessary participant for some topics or meetings, then schedule a discussion with the meeting owner to discuss how you could exit the meeting, meet their objectives another way, or only attend for specific relevant topics.

It can be difficult telling people you are not coming to their meetings as they can sometimes take it personally. Look for ways to meet their needs outside the meeting.

Why not suggest that they try applying these concepts themselves so that they can understand why you are disengaging and apply this to their meetings as well?

Trigger an action

Open your diary and make a note on the date of your next team meeting or after your next important meeting to discuss unnecessary participants. When the diary reminder pops up you will remember this chapter and be more likely to give the idea a try.

Discuss this with your team or at your next meeting

- Use and review your meetings tick chart to identify participation levels
- How do people participate at your meetings? Does this indicate that some people do not find some or all the topics relevant? Does everyone need to attend for every topic?
- Are there any unnecessary participant behaviors in your meeting? How can you deal with these?

- Discuss who needs to be on the bus or who is non-core and does not need to attend except by request when needed
- Identify people who could be consulted before the meeting or informed after the meeting and therefore do not need to attend the meeting itself

It is particularly useful to have this discussion when kicking off a new year or major activity, or when a new leader for the meeting or team is appointed. These are good opportunities to refine your way of working together.

PART 3

Designing much better meetings

. . .

By now you should have killed unnecessary topics and removed unnecessary participants from your meetings. You should also have a good idea of the topics that are relevant to all the participants in your meeting – and the ones that are not.

If you have not applied the learnings from Part 2 yet we strongly suggest doing this first; otherwise you will just be doing a better job of designing meetings that do not need to happen in the first place!

In this next section, we will look at planning and designing the meetings that **do** need to happen.

A lot of the success of meetings lies in getting the design right in advance. This is particularly important in virtual meetings where creating engagement spontaneously is much more difficult.

We will learn how to design OPPT meetings (driven by Outcomes, Process, Participation, and Timing) and solve two common meeting problems: unclear and slow decision-making; and too much information-giving.

There are significant opportunities to speed up and simplify your essential meetings to deliver their outcomes much more quickly and with fewer, more engaged people, both face to face and online. You can expect a further 20 percent or more improvement in your meetings by applying these tools.

We will also look at the added challenges of running global meetings and large events.

....

Chapter 6

What is your purpose?

 Actions – develop a clear, unique purpose for your overall meeting

 Target – be clear about what your meeting is for, and what it is not for at a high level, enabling you to focus your future agendas

The purpose of ad hoc meetings will be defined by the outcomes required. These meetings come together for a specific short-term focus and then disband. Chapter 7 will help you define clear outcomes and process for these.

Regular meetings, however, should have a definite, unique purpose and reason for existing – otherwise how can you know what topics should be on the agenda?

The only real reason to have a meeting is to do something collectively that you could not achieve on your own

For team meetings, this should flow from your team purpose and incorporate the elements of your team purpose that need to be delivered collaboratively.

- **Who is the collective?** Is it a team, a project, a department, a business activity? Start by naming the group, the team, or activity that this meeting specifically is designed to support
- **What are the things that need doing?** Be clear about what you will be doing in the meeting (and that this is an appropriate reason for meeting); good purposes include making decisions, learning, creating ideas, celebration, problem-solving, or improving ways of working. Poor purposes include sharing information, individual updates, or presentations where there is no role for participants
- **Be more specific**: to do what exactly? E.g. Make decisions on prioritization of the production schedule
- **What unnecessary topics intrude?** Ask your participants what kind of topics regularly come up in your meetings that should **not** be discussed there. We find people are usually very good at identifying the topics that slow things down or add little value
- **What interaction does it require that means this cannot be done alone?** If it is just people doing their day-to-day jobs, let them get on with it. If they need others to collaborate, create, or decide, you may need a meeting

- **What kinds of outcomes and actions will the meeting produce?** If there are no outcomes or actions, you do not need a meeting
- **How will we know when we have finished?** If the meeting is for a specific project or activity, set a deadline or success criteria that mean you can disband the meeting once you have achieved them

Discuss these questions with your team meeting participants to try to identify a clear, common, unique purpose for your meetings that is differentiated from other meetings in the business and makes it clear what kind of subjects you should be discussing.

Do not forget to check your ideas with any key stakeholders who are critical to the success of the meeting.

It is a good idea to show this purpose statement at the top of each future meeting agenda.

Do not be surprised if you find it difficult to immediately identify a clear purpose; it can take some time and discussion to clarify this.

If you can't establish a clear purpose for your meeting, then it probably does not need to be a regular meeting. It can happen that, once regular meetings are in people's diaries, they take on a life of their own. You will know this is happening when you are struggling to find items to fill the agenda.

If this is the case, cancel the regular meeting and just call ad hoc meetings when you have sufficient need in this area. If you have accidentally canceled a valuable meeting or topic people will soon come and ask to have it reinstated.

It is a good practice anyway to have at least an annual review of regular meetings to see if they are still fulfilling their purpose, if the purpose has changed, or if the meeting can be canceled.

A clear meeting purpose is essential in deciding what topics you should accept on the agenda and who should be invited. If the topics do not relate to the purpose of the meeting, then perhaps they should be discussed at a different meeting?

This is also another opportunity to check you are focusing on the spaghetti and to evaluate whether you have the right people attending the meeting to deliver the purpose. If not, you may need to revisit your purpose and the participants you invite.

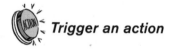 *Trigger an action*

Schedule some time in your diary to clarify the purpose of your meeting. Set a date at year end to review all your meetings.

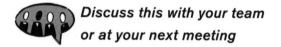 *Discuss this with your team or at your next meeting*

- What is the unique, differentiated purpose of this specific meeting?
- What kind of topics should be discussed here, and what should not?
- Does this need to be a regular or an ad hoc meeting?

Chapter 7

Drive outcomes and process, not agendas

. . . .

 Actions – plan and run a meeting using the OPPT
meeting format

 Target – improve the relevance and quality of the
outcomes and process of your meeting by at least
20 percent

. . . .

In Chapters 3–5 we focused on eliminating unnecessary meet-ings, topics, and participants.

By now you should have a more focused agenda based on topics that are relevant to all attendees. If not, we suggest you go back and complete the previous three steps first.

This chapter is about focusing your meeting topics on **outcomes and process** to make them more action-oriented and to ensure that practical outcomes are delivered. It will also start you thinking about designing in higher levels of participation and engagement – the focus of our next chapter.

Traditional meeting agendas often consist of a list of topics.

Unfortunately, when we see a topic title like "business review" it is not clear what output we want from the discussion. It could just be a presentation, we could be asked to give input, discuss options, or decide.

If you have a particularly difficult or regular meeting in mind that you want to improve, this would be a good time to **print off a copy of the agenda and have it next to you** as you read this chapter to see how it compares with the guidelines below.

A 2003 survey of senior leaders from 187 companies by Macron Intelligence found:

- Agenda setting is often loose and unfocused
- At half the companies surveyed, the agenda was the same from meeting to meeting or was ad hoc
- When asked about what got on to the agenda, participants said that it was usually driven by a crisis in one area, historical precedent (every November we review HR) or "fairness" (everyone should get a chance to speak)
- No one was explicitly in charge of looking after the agenda, with items often being added on a "first come, first served" basis
- Only 5 percent of companies had a system for rigorously directing management's time to the most important issues
- As little as 20 percent of senior management time was spent on topics that drive value for the company

Given these results, it is hardly surprising that most agendas are so poor.

Put someone in charge

Meetings are such an important part of collaboration and decision-making and are so expensive that it is surprising we do not put more effort into planning and running them. Often an administrator oversees the agenda and just asks attendees if they would like to add anything.

A relatively junior person who may not have the approval responsibility to spend money in other areas can easily call a meeting costing thousands of dollars.

Some, usually more expensive, meetings do have facilitators but often they focus on the behaviors in the meeting rather than on the focus, design, and outputs of the meeting.

If you are serious about improving your meeting, appoint someone to an active role in the planning and management of the meeting. Make sure they read this book.

Start with outcomes and process, not lists of agenda topics

By focusing on outcomes and process we make our meetings much more likely to produce concrete actions and clear decisions.

It will also help clarify who should attend the meeting (and who should not) and you can design in better facilitation and higher levels of participation and engagement.

It is particularly important to be clear about outcomes and process in conference calls and web meetings where it can be harder for participants to understand their roles and what input is expected; it is also easier for them to disengage without you realizing.

ANALYZE YOUR EXISTING MEETINGS

To see how your existing meetings compare with this approach, at the next meeting you attend make a note for each topic on whether they pass the OPPT test.

1. Was the **O**utcome explicitly stated in the agenda or at the beginning of the topic and was the outcome met?
2. Did you follow an explicit **P**rocess and did that process lead successfully to the outcome?
3. Were the right **P**articipants present in the meeting to deliver the outcome and follow the process?
4. Did you spend an appropriate amount of **T**ime on the topic?

Your observations on these questions will help improve your understanding of how being clear about these factors will improve your meeting.

THE OUTCOME-BASED MEETING PLANNER

Having observed a meeting without this structure, now use it to plan your next meeting.

This simple tool takes us through a four-part process for planning more effective OPPT meetings, calls, and webinars:

1. What outcomes do we want from each meeting topic?
2. What process will we need to deliver this outcome?

3. Which participants need to be involved?
4. How much time is it worth spending on this?

WHAT **O**UTCOMES DO WE WANT?	WHAT **P**ROCESS STEPS WILL WE FOLLOW?	WHICH **P**ARTICIPANTS NEED TO BE THERE?	HOW MUCH **T**IME IS IT WORTH SPENDING ON THIS?

1. What *outcome* do we want from this topic?

"We spent an hour discussing one issue and then at the end we found out that the decision had already been made and they were just informing us of it – I wish we had known that at the start, what a waste of time."

Sales operations coordinator, IT, USA

Begin by being clear about the outcome you want from having this topic on the agenda.

Typical outcomes may be:

- To make a specific decision
- To generate ideas and a solution to a specific problem
- To develop a plan of action for a specific situation

The outcome should define what will happen at the end of the discussion of the topic: what action, behavior change, or result do we expect to see?

If your first ideas about outcomes include "sharing information" or "listening to a presentation" please review the information in Chapter 4 and reconsider whether these topics need a meeting or just an email. Ask yourself the follow-up question **"In order to do what?"** to get closer to a practical outcome.

If the outcomes do not need participants to **do** anything differently, then consider alternatives to having them on your meeting agenda. The outcome should be something that needs live "synchronous" involvement of participants.

Example of a practical outcome: *Decide which vendor to choose for a specific purchase.*

2. What *process* will we need to deliver this outcome?

Once we are clear about the outcome, we can then define the process steps we will need to deliver that outcome. If this includes some sharing of information, please consider how this can be done before the meeting in pre-reading materials (see Chapter 9 for more on this). A robust process should lead you inevitably to the required outcome.

Example: If the outcome is to "decide which vendor to choose" the process may be:

- Discuss and agree the selection criteria
- Discuss the three leading vendors and rank them against the criteria
- Decide based on the ranking or by majority voting if the ranking is not conclusive

At this stage, it is useful to stop and consider two questions:

- Will this process deliver the outcome? If not, you need to re-plan the process
- Is this a "star" or "spaghetti" topic? (See above for definitions of these terms.) Do I really need a live meeting, call or webinar to achieve the outcome?

3. Which *participants* need to be involved and when to deliver this outcome?

Based on a clear outcome and process, it is normally easy to see who needs to be involved. Some will be obvious. Others may be key stakeholders with decision rights or people who need to formally agree the resources necessary to successful implementation.

If you are familiar with RACI analysis for clarifying roles (where you identify who is **R**esponsible, **A**ccountable, **C**onsulted, or **I**nformed for a given task of decision), be careful with how you involve the Cs and Is.

- "Consulted" is someone you ask before deciding
- "Informed" is someone you will tell after you have decided

You can consult and inform outside your meetings and these individuals do not necessarily need to attend the meeting itself. This will keep your meeting size smaller, and smaller meetings are usually better meetings.

This may, however, mean you need to spend more time outside the meeting on stakeholder engagement before and communication of actions afterwards.

If you are not familiar with RACI a simple online search will throw up many examples and formats.

You should have a clear owner who is responsible for the delivery and success of each outcome.

Each section of the agenda may need different participants to reach the outcome and follow the process.

4. *How much time* is it worth spending on this?

If you have ever spent hours discussing a trivial matter, you will know how frustrating this can be.

Given the costs of your meeting and the number of outcomes you want to deliver, you may have a limited amount of time you are willing or able to spend on a topic – be clear about this in advance.

Some topics are so important that if we spent the whole meeting delivering that one outcome, it would be a good use of our time. Others may be worth no more than a few minutes.

By having an initial time allocation, you can use this to facilitate during the meeting. When you are approaching the allocated time, ask, "We have already nearly used the time we allocated for this outcome; is it worth continuing or should we move on?" This often stops unnecessarily long discussions on low-value topics.

If you can calculate the value of your outcomes, it should be clear how much time and effort you should put into delivering them.

Use the OPPT meeting planner above to plan your next meeting, call, or webinar using these principles.

At the meeting, add a column to evaluate how well you met your outcomes and followed your process, whether the right people were involved, and whether you hit your planned timings. Use this to think about how you can continue to improve the planning and execution of your meetings.

As you start to use this template you can also give it to other people who wish to present at your meeting or add a topic. Make sure they are clear about the four OPPT steps in planning their session, ask to see their plan before the meeting and give them feedback on how well they followed their plan in the meeting itself.

WHAT OUTCOMES DO WE WANT?	WHAT PROCESS STEPS WILL WE FOLLOW?	WHICH PARTICIPANTS NEED TO BE THERE?	HOW MUCH TIME IS IT WORTH SPENDING ON THIS?	HOW WELL DID WE FOLLOW OUR PLAN – WHAT COULD WE IMPROVE NEXT TIME?

Use the final column of the planner to record your observations about how well you followed your plan.

- Were the outcomes clearly stated and were they met?
- Was the process explicit and followed as planned?
- Did we have the right participants involved?
- Did we stick to our timings?

If not, what do we need to do differently next time?

Designing for relevance

The best meetings are ones where the outcome is relevant to us and the process gets us to the outcome efficiently.

Unfortunately, the process of many meetings is to share too much information in the hope that something useful will fall out. In complex organizations today we have access to so much information it can sometimes be difficult to identify what is relevant from the mass of data.

We call this process "panning for gold." It is a bit like the old-time gold prospectors going into a stream and looking for nuggets of gold: if we are not focused we spend our whole life looking at mud and never find the nuggets; if we do not pay enough attention then the nuggets may fall through our hands. The trick is in paying attention to the right things.

Example: The budget review

I attended a management meeting with one of our clients to observe them in the morning, after which I would run a workshop in the afternoon.

In the morning, it was not clear to me what the outcome of the session was. The process they followed was for everyone to go through their budgets line by line to identify if there were any possible savings. The process took most of the morning and was painfully slow; a lot of the discussion was individuals defending why specific budgets could not be cut.

Over lunch the CEO asked me for my comments and I asked what outcome he was looking for. It may have been obvious to the attendees but it was not obvious to me. He

replied that there was a $5 million gap between the latest busi-
ness position and what they needed to achieve on costs.

I suggested that the process may be too detailed to get effi-
ciently to the outcome he wanted.

After lunch, I opened the discussion by asking the partici-
pants if they knew that the outcome of the session was to find
$5 million in savings. They replied that they did.

I told them that I presumed they had done some prepara-
tion before the meeting so I stood at a flipchart and asked
them to shout out who had got budget that could close this
gap. Within about five minutes we found the $5 million.

Once you are very clear about the outcome, it usually possible to
design a process to get more quickly to the outcome. Resist the
need to share everything and try to get to the point.

Example: The HR best practice meeting

An Americas HR team of 12 people held regular best practice
reviews where human resources people based from Canada to
Chile would present their learning to colleagues doing similar
jobs. Even at 15 minutes per presentation, this took three hours
of their valuable face-to-face team meeting and it frequently
overran. People often struggled to think of something they
wanted to share and usually ended up sharing something they
were proud of rather than anything that was useful to the others.

Participants found little value in this but the HR vice-presi-
dent was keen to transfer learning between the individuals.

We redesigned the meeting around "wants and offers"; we
asked each participant to prepare a flipchart with two
columns. The first column was "wants" – areas where they

were looking for ideas and learning to solve a problem they were facing. The second column was "offers" – areas where they thought they had a great idea to share with others.

After this first stage, we observed there were a lot more offers than wants – people were much more likely to offer their good ideas than to ask for help.

Next, we asked people to walk around all the flipcharts and mark their initials against the "offers" they were interested in finding out more about, and against any "want" that they thought they could help with.

After the second stage, there was very little interest in most of the offers. Only three of the offers had more than one person interested in them. However, lots of people thought they could help with other people's problems!

We asked the people who were interested in the three offers to form small teams to discuss them. Where there was only one person with an offer to help someone with a want, we asked them to schedule a one-to-one conversation later. Most of the smaller conversations happened outside the meeting either in breaks or later on the telephone.

After 30 minutes, the best practice reviews were finished and during that period people had only been involved in conversations they had chosen to join because they had an interest or a need.

Including preparation time, this process took 45 minutes, instead of the three hours it used to take. People's satisfaction with the quality and relevance of the discussions went up significantly.

Again, the trick was to design a process that delivers the outcome quickly and improves relevance and engagement for participants.

Trigger an action

Look ahead to the next important meeting that you are running. Schedule some time in your diary two weeks before the meeting for a planning session based around this chapter.

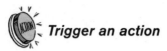 **Discuss this with your team or at your next meeting**

- Review your most regular or time-consuming meeting, conference call, or webinar
- Use the OPPT process to re-engineer it; how different would it look?
- Produce an outline agenda for each of the planned topics using the OPPT headings and use it to run your next meeting or call
- Be explicit with the meeting participants about what you are doing and why
- At the end of the meeting evaluate the impact it had on the conduct of the meeting and the quality of the outputs
- If it works for you, keep doing it!

Chapter 8

Improving the participant experience

 Actions – design and run your meeting for significantly higher levels of participation and engagement

 Target – improve the active engagement of your meeting participants by 25 percent

In many traditional meetings, we spend a significant amount of the time listening to presentations or broadcasts of information. Without active participation, meetings can become boring and passive.

A survey by Atlassian software of meeting attendees in the US found:

- 91 percent had daydreamed in meetings
- 39 percent had fallen asleep at least once
- 73 percent did other work

Another survey by RoperASW and Tandberg in 2003 sampled 625 business professionals in the USA, UK, Norway, Germany, and Hong Kong. They asked them what else they were doing while attending meetings.

During audio conferences	During face-to-face meetings
23% gave full attention to the audio conference	55% gave full attention
27% did other work	5% did other work
25% checked or did emails	3% checked or did emails
13% surfed the web	1% surfed the web
13% daydreamed	15% daydreamed

Our favorite finding was that in audio conferences 8 percent were not fully dressed!

This is not a great endorsement of the quality of the typical participant experience.

It is easy to fall into the trap of focusing on the presenter or meeting leader when they are the minority of attendees at the meeting. To get the best out of our meetings we need to think about the **participant experience.**

We never met anyone in our training programs who said, "I wish we had more meetings and presentations to look at," but many people do ask for more real conversations with their boss and close colleagues. Building real engagement means creating two-way communication where people can be listened to, interact, discuss, and ask questions.

It also means designing in opportunities to actively take part in the creation and development of ideas and decisions, rather than being told about the ideas and decisions of other people.

Active engagement increases buy-in and job satisfaction and leads to much more enjoyable meetings.

Conversely, if there is no role for participation, then it is likely that you could send information through a technology like email instead. You certainly do not need a live, synchronous meeting, call, or webinar to do this.

Where your meetings are conducted through technology, building participation is even more challenging and important as it is harder to read the body language clues that tell us whether people are engaged. If you do not engage people in virtual meetings it is very likely that they are multitasking or they may even log in and then walk away.

Start by improving participation in your face-to-face meetings. If they are boring and lack participation, then translating them to online tools will just mean that you can bore a larger population of people at a slightly lower cost!

In this chapter, we will show you how to improve participation and engagement both on- and offline by:

- Understanding the principles of participation
- Learning what is different in conference calls and web meetings
- Applying some online participation techniques
- Planning your meetings for participation

Principles of participation

At Global Integration, we put a lot of focus into creating participation and engagement in our face-to-face workshops and we have successfully applied these same principles to creating participation in conference calls and web conferences and even in our online learning where short bite-sized videos, downloadable worksheets, peer-to-peer sharing, comments, active moderation, and a leader board to encourage competition bring much more interactivity than traditional "PowerPoint-like" e-learning.

Here are our top seven principles for encouraging participation on- and offline:

1. **Focus on the audience**: usually there is only one presenter or leader but many more participants. Good questions to ask yourself include:
   - Do they all need to be there?
   - Does the topic need a live meeting or could we just send the information instead?
   - Is the session a good use of their time? Is the content relevant and engaging?
   - What is the outcome I need from these people?
   - What do I want them to know, do, or feel because of this session?
2. **For each outcome and process step ask, "What are the participants doing? How can we make it participative?"** Check what participants are doing at each stage of the process. If the answer is "shutting up and listening to me," then reconsider. Give them an active role
3. **Keep groups small**: smaller audiences allow for and encourage greater participation; if you want real interaction keep audiences down to six or seven people, particularly in virtual meetings. Conversely if you have large numbers of participants, say 15 or more, then it is very likely that you are using the meeting for star group

(broadcast) reasons or that you have several potential sub-teams in the same room. Try using other media or separate sub-team meetings instead of such a large meeting

4. **Encourage early participation**: if you present for two hours where participants have no role but to sit and listen, do not be surprised if you get few questions and little interaction at the end – you have trained them to remain silent and passive. Get participants doing something active within four minutes

5. **Involve people in the generation and creation of materials and ideas** rather than just presenting finished ideas and materials to them. Get people to write on flipcharts, screens, Post-it notes, whiteboards, or other materials and come up with their own ideas and solutions

6. **Engage all the senses**: use colour and music – even smell. Encourage movement by getting people to walk around and post things on the walls. In conference calls and webinars, have regular breaks for movement

7. **Make the room layout match the process of the meeting**: if you walk into a darkened room with rows of chairs facing a brightly lit stage, the message is clear – you are here to listen and not distract the presenter at the front. Small round tables encourage participation and group discussion. If the "room" is virtual, keep numbers small, build in regular opportunities for interaction, and provide for subgroups and breakout sessions

If you find that there is little role for participation in your meeting, then why not cancel it and send an email with an attachment of your content instead?

WHY DO YOU NEED ICEBREAKERS?

Our clients sometimes ask us to suggest "icebreakers" for their events or workshops. We ask, "What have you done to create ice?"

If the content is engaging and participative you do not need icebreakers – the ice never formed in the first place.

If people are meeting for the first time and you want them to get to know each other quickly then build in time for introductions or get them straight into doing something relevant to the topic together.

Conference call and online meeting participation tips

We can take the principles and philosophies behind these ideas and apply them to our virtual meetings.

Here are some additional tips:

- **Master the technology**: in creating participation online, we need to understand the technology and the opportunities it gives us. Most web conferencing tools, for example, offer significant opportunities for us to create engagement and participation – but only if we plan for them in advance. It is very difficult to create spontaneous participation with these tools.

   Check that your people have been trained in the technology you use. It is quite common in our workshops to find that, in an organization that actively uses tools like WebEx or Skype for Business, for example, fewer than 20 percent of the people have ever been formally trained to use the system.

When we run webinars ourselves, many of the attendees have trouble logging in and using the basic functionality of the tools, suggesting they have never used them before.

Most providers of these systems give access to free or inexpensive online training and you can usually learn all you need to know in about 45 minutes.

If people are not aware of the technical opportunities and limitations of the tool there will always be this barrier to communication. Get the knowledge barrier out of the way early by insisting that people are trained in the tools

- **Plan to use the participation tools regularly**: once you have overcome the technology barrier, the key challenge is in creating engagement and participation.

  Preparation for online engagement does take longer but with a little planning you can incorporate some or all the following tools into the way you run your online events

Here are our top 11 participation and engagement tools for online meetings:

1. **Ask questions by name**: ask different specific individuals questions, particularly if you have not heard from them yet. By doing this regularly you will set the expectation that people are paying attention as they could be called on at any time
2. **Polling**: you can ask a question and give real-time feedback on the results. Example: "How satisfied were you with this meeting?" This also helps lower the barrier to giving and receiving the immediate feedback many younger people value

3. **Voting**: either through a "raise your hand" or yes/no function in most webinar tools. Example: "Have you received the new organization announcement?"

4. **Subgroups**: in some systems you can set up subgroups and give them each a separate conference call number so they can have side discussions and report back to the main group. Example: "Team A, please consider your answer to question 1 and create a slide of your ideas to share with us when we resume as a full group in ten minutes; team B, take question 2." Smaller subgroups improve participation levels

5. **Screen sharing**: you can break a presentation slide into several segments and ask individuals to type their responses or use other annotation tools such as pens or shapes on the screen; for example, "Type what you see as the advantages of this idea in the top left quadrant, and the disadvantages in the bottom right quadrant"

6. **Hand over control**: allow individuals to take control of segments and add their comments or inputs or share documents or applications

7. **Take regular breaks**: we recommend no more than an hour of continuous webinar or conference call. Participation levels fall fast if online events or calls go on too long. For cross-cultural, multilingual groups make breaks even more frequent to give people time to process the material and rest. Taking part in a second or third language is tiring

8. **Enable questions**: have a mechanism for asking questions, either by the "raise your hand" function or through chat. It is quite hard to check chat or questions

while running a large webinar, so it is useful to have a colleague who checks these for you and feeds you any specific questions that need to be answered during the breaks. Pause regularly and ask for questions or check the chat box

9. **Use materials that call for interaction**: get participants to fill in slides, use their pointer or annotation tools and type answers to questions so that they have some physical activity to perform rather than falling back into the passive viewing of content that someone else has created

10. **Limit audience size**: the larger the audience the easier it is to hide and the harder it is to involve everyone. You should limit participation to the least number of people needed to meet your goal. If you need real (spaghetti) teamwork online, limit the audience to three to six participants

11. **Integrate other media**: share documents in advance and set up a social space to continue the discussion and ask questions afterwards. Your younger managers may well have used these tools outside work and can be a great source of ideas about how to create engagement online. Ask them to help design the process to increase interaction

As you design your session, build a variety of these tools into the process; you should plan to engage early and then every four or five minutes to keep participants' attention and engagement.

Note: not all these tools are included in every web meeting system – learn what exists in your specific one.

TOP 11 ENGAGEMENT TOOLS: PLANNING SHEET

Tool	How can you use this in your virtual meeting?
Ask questions by name	
Polling	
Voting	
Subgroups	
Screen sharing	
Handing over control	
Take regular breaks	
Enable questions	
Use materials that call for interaction	
Limit audience size	
Using social media or other tools around the meetings	

In our "Compelling virtual facilitation" webinar training we usually begin by showing the tools that we will ask participants to use during the workshop. Many of them have never had the opportunity to participate online before and are amazed at what you can do if you integrate and use the participation tools intelligently.

We then go on to train people to design and run much more engaging virtual meetings by using these tools regularly to keep audiences alert and participating.

THE VIRTUAL MEETING TABLE

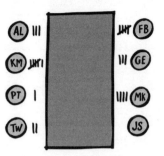

The virtual meeting table is a simple tool for managing participation. Simply draw a table shape on a piece of paper and make a note around it of the names of the participants. You can do this for face-to-face meetings, audio, web, or video conferences.

In the same way as you did for the meetings tick chart in Chapter 4, each time someone speaks, make a check mark against their name.

If you are meeting by audio conference you may need to ask people to introduce themselves each time they speak to help with this – this is a good practice anyway if people do not know each other well enough to recognize voices.

On most web tools, you should be able to see who is speaking by the microphone highlight next to their name or the fact that their video feed becomes the primary one.

As you do this you will quickly see who has spoken and who has not.

Give participants a task or interaction that requires an individual response within the first four minutes. This also prevents individuals multitasking or quietly leaving the meeting as they then expect to be called on.

As the meeting progresses, make a point of asking questions of those who have not yet responded and involve them in the meeting.

If someone is dominating the conversation it may be worth sending them a direct message or chat asking them to let others contribute too, or speaking to them afterwards about moderating their level of input.

By making sure everyone is expected to and has a chance to speak you will set an expectation that people will be paying attention and contributing.

If there are important decisions to be made or topics on which you want everyone to contribute, you can use the virtual meeting table to go around systematically to make sure everyone has expressed an opinion or agreed to the decision.

Try to build in an opportunity to participate actively every four to five minutes. Use a variety of techniques rather than the same ones repeatedly.

Remember to plan participation and engagement in advance by concentrating on the participant experience. If you simply use tools like WebEx or Skype for Business as online page-turners to give presentations, you will find that people are not really paying attention.

In face-to-face meetings, we may have to pretend to look interested for reasons of politics or politeness. If an online presentation is boring, we will do our emails or check Facebook instead.

CHECK YOUR PARTICIPATION OPPORTUNITIES

To evaluate how many opportunities people have to participate during the existing meetings you run or attend, record the frequency and variety of opportunities for people to participate actively during each agenda item. Typical participation activities might include:

- Asking questions
- Filling in flipcharts or wall-charts
- Moving around to add to materials
- Writing or creating shared documents
- Discussing actively
- Making a decision
- Voting, polling, questions, or other participation on web meetings

Be specific on timings and content so you can capture the range of activities participants were involved in.

DESIGN FOR FLOW AND ENERGY

Participation and engagement demand energy and energy is hard to sustain at high levels for long periods of time. As well as taking regular breaks there are things you can do to design in the right level of energy in the flow of your meetings.

- Avoid habituation. If every topic consists of the same process, for example a discussion, recording on a flipchart and voting, then people will soon get bored. Mix up the way people participate, get them moving, use Post-its, mix up the groups and find different ways to run the process
- Start with a topic where you are very likely to succeed. Give the meeting a quick win and make them feel good

- Have your most important item second to make sure that you give plenty of time for it to be completed and to ensure any late arrivers are there by then
- If you have a controversial or high-energy topic, follow it with something simpler to allow people to recover energy levels
- If the topic is going nowhere and you are unlikely to reach your outcome, park it and come back to it later or at another meeting
- If you are using subgroup discussions, mix up the membership regularly
- After every break in a face-to-face meeting get people to sit in a different place to give a different perspective and an opportunity to work with different colleagues

It is easy to evaluate the level of energy in a face-to-face meeting – just look around at people's faces. Do they look engaged, are they paying attention, or checking their emails? If they look bored and inactive, they probably are.

On a conference call, you will feel the energy levels by how actively people contribute. On WebEx, presenters can see an "attention meter" that shows how many people are multitasking. If you mention this from time to time – "I can see that a couple of people are multitasking" – people usually stop quickly.

If energy levels seem low, then flag it as an issue. Say, "The energy level seems to have gone down, what shall we do about it?" And then propose a change of state – take a break, do something different, or ask the participants for ideas about how you could bring the energy back up again.

UPDATE YOUR MEETINGS PLANNER

In Chapter 7 you used the meeting planning tool to focus on outcomes, process, participants, and timing – the first four columns below. Now we add a fifth column, "what will participants be doing?", to check you have designed in opportunities for active participation and engagement.

Remember, if there is no active role for participants, you probably do not need a meeting.

WHAT **O**UTCOMES DO WE WANT?	WHAT **P**ROCESS STEPS WILL WE FOLLOW?	WHICH **P**ARTICIPANTS NEED TO BE THERE?	HOW MUCH **T**IME IS IT WORTH SPENDING ON THIS?	WHAT WILL THE PARTICIPANTS BE DOING?

When you are using this format to plan a virtual meeting, include in the final column notes about which of the online participation tools participants will be using at each stage.

Make sure that you have built time for these into your materials and make notes on how and when you will use these tools. Some, such as polls, you will need to prepare in advance.

"I was invited to a meeting and then we spent the whole time watching a video. I could have done that at home. If I am going to give up valuable time for a meeting, I expect to have a role."

R&D manager, pharmaceuticals, USA

Example: Large virtual meetings

It is particularly difficult to create interaction online with very large groups. People may use the anonymity of being part of a large audience that is invisible to the facilitator to multitask or just ignore the content.

One of our clients in the pharmaceutical industry used to run a large functional WebEx session with over 1,000 attendees every quarter. These calls were often run at times that were not particularly convenient for participants outside the USA.

The session consisted of broadcasting information that the functional head thought was useful. As we have seen, finding "spaghetti" topics that are relevant to over 1,000 people is extremely difficult.

I asked the senior leader how many people turned up to the call and he told me that everybody did as he had put a lot of effort into encouraging attendance. I was skeptical, so after ten minutes I ran a quick poll to find out how many people were present and paying attention; more than a third of the people appeared to have logged on and then left – which is a rational response if the call is in the middle of the night and not very relevant to you.

We ran a survey to find out what the participants thought was most relevant for a call of this type. They initially said that the calls were too regular (which is normally a sign that people do not think it is useful).

They told us that they found the central updates useful in giving them an overview of what was happening at HQ. Although this was a classic star group broadcast and something that could be sent out by email, people did find it helpful.

The functional head decided he could record a video or WebEx session on that part of the message and send it to people so that they could view it at a more convenient time. He would then only take specific questions about the content on the call.

Another goal was to create a sense of community. This is extremely hard to do when working through technology with very large groups and we suggested that it might be better to have smaller speciality groups sharing information in more manageable group sizes. There were a few specialist group communities that formed around the need to stay updated on, for example, learning and development or organization development. These groups had far more relevant information to share.

Some of the groups decided to run two webinars with the same content so that people could select the time that was best for their own time zones.

Another useful element for large communities that could not get together was recognition and celebration of success, where individuals or teams were recognized for an achievement.

For the slimmed-down and more relevant webinar we used the participation tools to engage people in collecting information through polls, capturing their views through use of arrows and whiteboards, calling out specific individuals with questions, and using the chat function to capture questions which we dealt with as we went along.

The principle was to engage the audience regularly to maintain their attention and to stop people multitasking or leaving the screen.

These large events remain a challenge; however, increased relevance and regular engagement can make a real difference even at this scale of meeting.

IT IS NOT ABOUT THE BEACH HUTS AND BASKETBALL HOOPS

We have seen some great meeting rooms from Silicon Valley to London and Romania. We have seen rooms themed as beach huts, ski lodges, boxing rings, and casinos. One of our favorites was a video conference room themed around the Tour de France where you have to cycle on fixed bikes facing the screen to power the system.

It is great to provide an attractive environment, particularly where the local teams themselves get to develop and implement the themes; this can give a real sense of ownership and pride in the facilities and act as an attractor for new hires.

Putting a basketball hoop in the corner of a dreadful meeting, however, does not make boring and irrelevant meeting content fun.

Particularly where we have an attractive meeting environment, we need to make the content of the meeting engaging and participative or the mismatch between the two will be very clear.

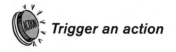 **Trigger an action**

Make a note in your diary to design your next important meeting around the participation principles.

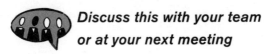 **Discuss this with your team
or at your next meeting**

Plan your next meeting around the participant experience. Design in increased opportunities to participate in an active way.

- Find out how to use the participation tools in your web meeting technology, and practice using them in your next online meeting
- Apply the participation principles to your design
- Ask participants how they felt about this more active way of engaging in meetings
- Ask them how else they would like to participate
- If it works for you, keep doing it!

Chapter 9

Faster, better decisions

Actions – identify the key decisions you make in your meetings and the best way to make them

Target – improve the way you make decisions in your meeting by reducing the number of people involved and clarifying decision rights and process

Many organizations are concerned that decisions take too long to make. As the pace of business continues to accelerate, we cannot afford slow decision-making.

A large proportion of everyday decisions are made in meetings so, by improving the way we make decisions in our meetings, we can speed up decision processes across the organization.

In our work with organizations around the world we find there are three critical challenges to improving decision-making in meetings:

1. Being clear about who has the right to make a decision
2. Being clear about how the decision will be made
3. Involving only the right people at the right time

There are, of course, other challenges in re-engineering large-scale decision processes such as, for example, the innovation process, or large-scale strategic decision-making; however these are outside the scope of this book.

Clarifying decision rights

As organizations become increasingly connected and integrated, work becomes more collaborative. It can easily become unclear who will be involved in decisions and what process we will need to follow. There is a tendency for more people than are necessary to be involved and for the process to become slow and bureaucratic.

> *"It is often not clear who needs to be involved to make a decision so it is easier to invite everyone to the meeting, just in case."*
>
> Finance manager, software industry, India

To clarify decision **rights** several of our clients use a variant of the RACI process known as DICE. Here we identify who plays the roles of Decision-maker, Informed, Consulted, and Execute in deciding.

Use this idea to discuss and agree who are the real decision-makers and, for others, be clear specifically what their role is in making a given decision.

If you do not do this in advance, many more people may assume they have a formal role in the decision.

If decision rights have been unclear for some time or have changed recently you may find that people are reluctant to give up their historic decision rights.

> *"We introduced a matrix structure and found that too many people were getting involved in decisions and not letting go of their legacy decision rights.*
>
> *For people who have been used to being at the center of decisions this can be hard. When we used DICE there was some reluctance by individuals who were not named as Ds to give up their role. Some accepted they were Cs but wanted to be labeled as 'strong Cs' so they would still be more involved. One of the people at the meeting shouted, 'For God's sake, give up your Ds.'"*
>
> VP, HR, packaged goods, Dubai

Clarifying the decision process

It is also useful to understand the decision-making **process** – what mechanism will be used to make the decision?

In simple terms, there are four main ways of making decisions and these link closely to our star and spaghetti models in Chapter 4.

Star groups tend to let the right individuals make the decisions.

1. **The boss decides.** This is a decision that should be made based on authority. It could be defined in the delegation

of authority rules of the organization or it may be something that the boss feels they need to reserve to themselves

2. **Collegiate decision.** In this style of decision-making the boss will consult others first but is responsible for making the final decision

3. **An empowered individual decides.** The decision is within the area of responsibility of an expert or someone with specific responsibility for this and the individual is empowered to make the decision themselves

These star group decisions are made based on expertise or role. **Spaghetti teams** tend to make decisions collectively:

4. **Collective decisions.** The decision-making unit is more than one person and therefore there needs to be a process of discussion and agreement. Most commonly, groups decide either through:
   a. consensus (everyone discusses and comes to a common view) *or*
   b. some form of voting (formal or informal), where the majority view holds sway

   These decisions are a collective process which may again be based on expertise and role rather than hierarchy or formal authority. However, they can often be based on whoever happens to be at the meeting (everyone gets a vote or a say in consensus) – which is not always a good reason for being a decision-maker

In clarifying decision rights, it is important to be transparent about who needs to be involved and which of these processes they will use to decide.

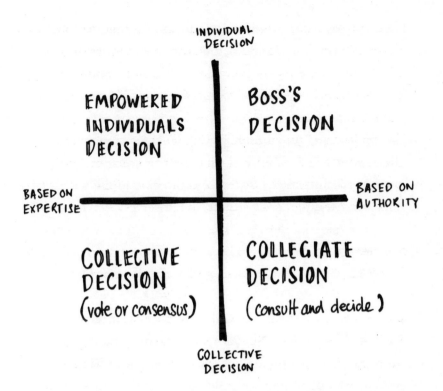

In a healthy meeting or team, decision-making should be able to flow to the individuals who have the expertise to make the decision, rather than just the positional authority.

> *"Why talk to someone with a job title, when you can talk to someone with an answer?"*
>
> Production manager, speciality materials, USA

In the absence of this clarity there is a tendency to default to collective decision-making which is slower and more complex. There are times when this is the right way to make decisions, but there are many more occasions when empowered individuals or smaller sub-teams will get the job done better and faster.

There are also some dangers in collective decision-making in areas where expertise should be the primary criteria.

"I sit on a team with several specialists in areas like regulatory affairs, medical, market access, and marketing. It appears the team has become the decision-making body for everything. One symptom of this is that we cannot seem to decide in between meetings. In some cases, I find myself voting on a proposal made by the content expert in an area. It cannot be right that the average of the views of the one person who does know and the six who do not is the way the decisions are taken!"

Marketing manager, pharmaceuticals, Denmark

There are some national cultural differences in preferences for decision-making styles. For example, Scandinavian cultures and Japan have a relative preference for consensus decision-making while hierarchy plays a bigger role in Latin and Arab cultures.

Even within cultures it is important to be clear how decisions will be made, though we will usually tend toward the style that works best locally.

In international meetings, however, being explicit about decision rights and process is essential as otherwise people will naturally bring their own cultural expectations and be frustrated when they are not met. By being explicit we help overcome misunderstanding and delays to decisions.

INVOLVING THE RIGHT PEOPLE AT THE RIGHT TIME

It is also worth being clear about the role of the C and the I.

Consulting is something you do before making a decision, to take into account the views of the Cs as you consider the issue.

Informing is something you do after you have decided.

Neither of these two roles is decision-maker itself, though if you involve them too much in the decision process they may assume that they are. It is important to be clear if you want to speed up your decision-making.

DECISION-MAKING AS DEVELOPMENT

Watching experienced people weigh judgments and make decisions is an important source of development for young managers. If we take some of this decision-making out of the collective arena, we need to help them understand why decisions were made and how decisions are made in the organization.

Making decision rights and processes more explicit may help young managers in some ways but we also need to make sure we communicate the reasons why important decisions were made and provide some coaching on context and how to exercise judgment around larger decisions.

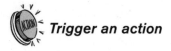 **Trigger an action**

Take some time to review how decisions are made in your meeting. Are decision rights clear and appropriate? Are the right people involved at the right time?

 Discuss this with your team or at your next meeting

Discuss these different ways of making decisions with your meeting participants.

Take one or more of the important or regular decisions you make at your meeting and discuss:

- How should these decisions be made in future?
- Who should make the decisions?
- If it is a collective decision, who has the expertise to be involved in making that decision?
- Apply your findings to a decision in your meeting and see if it works for you.

Further resources: this chapter is based on an extract from our book *Making the Matrix Work* from the section about creating clarity and making difficult decisions. You will find more there about managing complex trade-offs and making complex decisions.

Chapter 10

Taking information-giving out of your meeting

 Actions – identify opportunities to cut information-sharing from your meeting and make better use of pre-reading

 Target – remove information-sharing entirely from at least one topic in your meetings in the next two weeks

Have you ever been to a meeting where:

- You received a 150-page PowerPoint deck of pre-reading full of complicated charts and unclear bullet points
- Your pre-reading arrived late at night for a meeting that started first thing in the morning
- You did the pre-reading but only half the people at the meeting had done it, so you had to go through the same information again in the meeting

- Someone presented the same information that was in the pre-reading in the meeting, even though people had already read it

These are common experiences. If we want to create more participative and engaging meetings, then one of the key ways we can do this is to take out the parts of the meeting that are not participative and engaging – these are usually the information-giving parts and commonly make up around 40 percent of a traditional meeting.

A 2003 survey of senior leaders in 187 companies by Macron Intelligence found that more than 65 percent of meetings were not set up to decide but instead were for "info sharing" or "status updates." These are classic star group topics that do not need a live meeting.

Bain & Company examined the time budgets of 17 large corporations and found that 80 percent of meetings were with colleagues in the same department, rather than cross-function-ally and a lot of those meetings were there for information-shar-ing rather than for decision-making.

Sometimes we need information to complete the value-added part of the meeting such as deciding. If this is the case then we need to find better ways to give the information in advance, such as through pre-reading, so we can focus the live meeting on the decision or debate itself.

Here are some principles on how to do this:

FOCUS YOUR PRE-READING CONTENT
Too often presenters will circulate a long standard PowerPoint deck about the topic with far too much detail and where it is not

clear what outcome they are expecting from the participants at the meeting.

Without a reasonable understanding of context and what we are being asked to do, how can we possibly prepare to participate?

Procter & Gamble are famous for using a **"one page memo"** format with five defined steps.

1. Summarize the situation: what is the context and background?
2. Introduce your idea briefly: what you are proposing
3. Explain how your idea works: the basic steps: how, what, who, when, where
4. Reinforce the idea's three key benefits that are relevant to the audience
5. Suggest the next step: what outcome are you expecting from the meeting participants to move things forward?

As the name suggests, the discipline is to do all this in one page. If you can achieve that then you have probably thought through very carefully what it is you want to accomplish from the meeting.

If you are clear about the outcome you want from the participants at the meeting, then you will help them to prepare and are much more likely to achieve your goals.

Let people know what you want them to do and then give them the information in advance that they will need to do it.

YOU CAN DISCUSS OUTSIDE THE MEETING, TOO

By using social technologies, we can not only share information but also have some of the initial discussion and idea-sharing online outside the meeting, too.

At Global Integration we share important documents in advance of the discussion on Huddle and ask for comments and revisions, so that when we do meet face to face we are only working on an advanced version of the idea or proposal.

Sometimes we find we do not need to meet at all but can do all the work asynchronously. On other occasions, for major changes, we feel the need to sit around the table, look each other in the eyes and formally agree.

Either way, socializing the ideas and proposals in advance helps people to prepare and allows us to have much more advanced discussions at our live meetings.

USE THE RIGHT TOOL

PowerPoint is a great tool for making presentations. It is designed to act as a backdrop to a verbal explanation of issues.

Good slide design includes using a small number of bullet points that we can then talk around in the presentation.

We can easily include complicated charts and graphs because we can explain the trends and point out issues with the chart visible in the background.

Unfortunately, having created this presentation, we then email it to people and expect them to understand the context, what to pay attention to and what we expect from them.

We do not believe that PowerPoint is the right tool to meet this objective. We would much rather receive a well-written one- or two-page summary of the issues as above.

If you do insist on using PowerPoint, make sure that there is enough information on the slides to be explicit about the outcome you expect and to deliver the information needed to reach this outcome. Be aware that if this extends to more than about ten slides it is unlikely people will have read it.

DO NOT RE-READ THE PRE-READ

"I used to do the pre-reading for our meetings, but then there was always one person who had not done it so we would have to go through the information live in the meeting anyway. I soon learned not to waste my time by preparing."

Project manager, telecoms, UK

By doing this you effectively punish the people who did the pre-reading.

Alternatively, we have also been to meetings where the pre-reading was circulated and read by everyone but then the presenter still insists on going through it all again live in the meeting. The people who did the pre-reading are bored – maybe they will not prepare next time either.

If you want to build the discipline of doing pre-reading correctly, then it is essential that you do not repeat the content in the meeting.

"In our meeting, if someone has not prepared, the meeting leader asks them to go and sit outside and return when they have done the pre-reading and can contribute. In the

meantime, the topic discussion continues without them. They usually only do this once."

Technical manager, materials, Netherlands

An alternative approach for companies where people are not disciplined enough to do pre-reading is to give a short amount of time at the beginning of every topic (up to five minutes) for everyone to do the relevant reading. This at least prevents long presentations as people usually read up about an issue much more quickly than it would take to give the information in a live presentation.

At the beginning of your meeting topic simply ask participants if they have any questions following the pre-reading.

PARTICIPANTS CONTROL HOW MUCH INFORMATION THEY RECEIVE – NOT THE PRESENTER

"As senior R&D leaders we regularly sit through large numbers of engineering presentations by very passionate engineers. They give us far too much information and we just cannot dedicate enough time to listen to everybody. We would much rather have conversations with them."

R&D director, food industry, France

When you give people time to present at your meeting they are normally, by far, the most enthusiastic person about that topic in the room. They usually take up more time than anyone else would prefer.

If you give an engineer the opportunity to present their current development or a project manager the chance to explain their current project, they will (at least) fill the time you gave to them. They will also probably give you much more information than you need and often the wrong kind of information.

You can deal with this by taking control over the information you receive rather than giving that responsibility to the presenter.

We worked with this R&D group to move to a "tradeshow" format instead. Each engineer was given a table for a sample and a flipchart for a poster in a large room.

The senior leaders then circulated around the room spending time with individuals depending on their personal level of interest or expertise in the project.

The engineers had an opportunity to present key information to small groups but in general the questions of the senior leaders drove the sessions.

By giving control of how much information they receive to the audience you reduce the amount of information-giving and improve engagement and participation by giving them a bigger role in these sessions.

USE TEMPLATES

We can waste a lot of time with pre-reading or presentations trying to understand different charts, definitions of figures, and formats.

If you can agree on a standard template that is used each time – for example for a business update – then people will become familiar with the format and the information they are being presented with and this will cut down the time it takes for them to assimilate and understand it.

SEND IT OUT EARLY

There is no point sending out pre-reading if people do not have time to read it.

Ideally pre-reading should be sent out a week before the meeting to give people time to prepare their views. If it is sent out less than 48 hours before, there is a good chance that people have other commitments and you may not get across the information you need to have an effective meeting.

If you cannot get the pre-reading out in good time, consider whether it would be better to delay your topic until the next meeting.

The purpose of all this is to take information-giving where possible out of the content of the meeting. This enables us to have more efficient, engaging, and participative meetings.

By being much more focused about the outcomes of the meeting and providing the context and information we need to deliver the outcome, we can also have much more effective discussions and quicker decisions.

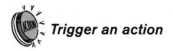 *Trigger an action*

Review how you use pre-reading and give information in your meeting. Think about how you can improve by applying the ideas in this chapter.

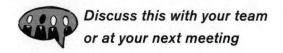

**Discuss this with your team
or at your next meeting**

- Discuss with your participants how you use pre-reading and information-sharing currently
- Set agreed expectations about how you will deal with this in future and build this into your next agenda
- Run at least one topic on your next meeting based on pre-reading that is not repeated in the meeting
- If/when people have not properly prepared, lead a discussion on this and reset expectations for next time
- Keep your focus on this and it will improve

Chapter 11

Taking your meetings global

Actions – understand what is different about running international meetings; identify and address the specific challenges relevant to your meeting

Target – if you have people from different cultures in your team, drive a discussion on the relevant topics in your next meeting

If you are running an international or global meeting, then you face additional challenges in working across different national cultures and time zones.

In this chapter, we summarize some of the key differences you will see in planning and running your meetings internationally or globally.

Please be aware that anything we say about another culture is also a reflection on ourselves. We notice most what is different from what we are used to, so any cultural observation is **50 percent about you and 50 percent about the other culture.** If you see another culture as informal, for example, this probably means you appear too formal to them.

Corporate and functional cultures and personality can also have an impact, so it is good to discuss the specific diversity in your meeting and come up with a solution that works best for you, rather than to rely on cultural averages or standard solutions.

If you work for an organization where international meetings are already common, you will probably already have some corporate cultural expectations and practices around meetings that overlay the national cultural preferences below. Even if this is the case it can be helpful to understand how people prefer to meet in their own cultures.

The cultural dimensions of meetings

Are meetings there to achieve tasks or to develop relationships?

This is not to say that meetings in task-oriented cultures do not pay attention to relationships or that relationship-oriented people do not achieve tasks; it is rather a question of where they start.

In more relationship-oriented cultures (found more commonly in Latin America, southern Europe, and Asia) the relationship needs to be strong **before** the task can be carried out. More task-oriented cultures (such as the USA and northern Europe) may suspend or ignore relationship issues, jump into dealing with the task at hand, and then get to know each other later.

Healthy meetings in all cultures successfully reconcile both needs. Even in the most task-oriented culture a meeting works better when personal relationships and trust are well established.

In general, make time in your cross-cultural meetings to ensure relationships are established and working before you launch into your tasks.

2. Level of formality

In some cultures (such as Japan or Germany) meetings tend to be more formal and structured and roles and responsibilities are relatively strictly defined; in others (such as in southern Europe or Latin America) meetings are more informal and freewheeling.

Regular meetings will usually develop their own norms on levels of formality. In a new meeting where people do not know each other it may be better to start by being relatively formal and allow the meeting to become more informal as people get to know each other.

Formal meeting cultures often expect a higher level of structure and process in a meeting than informal cultures. Discuss what works best for your meeting.

3. Are meetings where we make decisions?

In some cultures (such as Japan) meetings are traditionally for the exchange of pre-prepared information and decisions and there is little expectation that these positions will be changed during the meeting.

This may reflect the fact that more senior stakeholders have mandated a position before the meeting. Alternatively, the view expressed may be the result of extensive preparation or consensus-building in the wider population of people affected by the issue or decision under discussion.

In any case the people coming to the meeting will need to present their findings back to the wider or more senior stakeholders before they can change their position and be confident about carrying the others with them.

In other cultures, particularly individualistic ones such as the UK and USA, people come to the meeting expecting to share information, synthesize new information immediately, and make decisions in the meeting. Participants from these cultures then "sell" these decisions to the wider population after the meeting. The meeting itself is the mechanism for making decisions; and once the individual has agreed, they will go off and convince or just inform the wider stakeholders.

"Synthesizers" may be frustrated by the need of "exchangers" to consult more widely but should beware of pushing for immediate decisions. Even if they get apparent agreement the decision may change following consultation outside the meeting.

Make sure you are clear and explicit about how you will handle this in your meetings. If you need to engage stakeholders outside the meeting you may need to do more stakeholder management and communication and be aware that the meeting is only a small part of the decision process, not the process itself.

4. How do we prepare for meetings?
There are distinct cultural differences in how people tend to prepare themselves for meetings, including:

* Whether they prepare
* How much detail they expect
* How much lobbying and discussion is done outside the meeting

In the UK we prefer being pragmatic and developing solutions in the meeting, which may lead us to undervalue preparation. In Germany, by contrast, a lack of preparation is likely to be seen as unprofessional.

In other cultures, such as Italy, a lot of decisions can be made faster informally outside the meeting over coffee and in the corridor.

It will usually be evident how the individuals in your meeting prepare. Some will arrive with piles of files and copies of all the past minutes, while others arrive at the last moment with a blank pad of paper.

To cope with the wide range of assumptions you may meet within cross-cultural meetings, it is sensible to allow for a range of styles and preferences.

Without an understanding of these differences this is an issue that can cause frustration. Individuals who have prepared thoroughly may feel that those who expect less preparation and more flexibility in the meeting itself are not taking the subject seriously. Those who prefer not to agree on everything in advance may feel that those who have prepared and lobbied are presenting a "fait accompli" that they have no opportunity to challenge.

Preparation becomes even more important when people are not working in their native language. Allowing time to read key documents in advance and think about the vocabulary needed to get across key points is always appreciated.

5. How direct is our communication?

Cross-cultural researchers use the idea of high- and low-context cultures to help understand these differences.

High-context cultures tend to communicate through many other signals as well as the words they use. To really understand the message, you need to understand the context. The context is established through indirect references, body language, tone, intonation, and "coded" language whose meaning may be different from the apparent meaning of the words.

Asian cultures tend to be very high context where indirect communication through suggestions, hints, and even silence may leave you to fill in the details for yourself.

In Europe, the English tend to be high context; rather than directly say they do not agree with something they may say "Interesting," or "Good idea, could I ask you a couple of questions?"

The purpose of the indirectness is usually to be polite and to avoid causing open conflict.

High-context communication is fine between people who share the contextual information needed to complete the communication. It is protective of relationships and polite, but it can be unclear.

High-context people need to make more of an effort to be clear and direct in international meetings.

Low-context cultures focus on the words they use to communicate. The meaning is in the words themselves and is less dependent on the surrounding context. Low-context cultures say what they mean in a direct way. Many Americans, Germans, and Dutch people tend to be more low context; if they do not agree they will say, "I do not agree."

Low-context communication is clear, direct, and unambiguous so the message gets across unmistakably. To high-context listeners, however, this may sound rude and rather superficial.

They may be shocked to be told "That is a bad idea," without an introduction on the reasons and the context in which this view has been formed.

Low-context speakers need to put more effort into being diplomatic and polite when talking to high-context colleagues.

To really understand high-context messages, you may need to spend time "getting the context," listening to things you may think are not relevant but will become clear later.

If people come from cultures that prefer high-context communication, then it follows that they normally prefer to be communicated with in a high-context way. If you are producing presentations or written inputs to the meeting, think about how you will get messages across to both ends of the context spectrum.

- High-context cultures will want to know how proposals have been arrived at and to understand the thinking and the surrounding circumstances
- Low-context cultures often want to get to the "bottom line" of the proposal as quickly as possible

A practical solution may be to give both a more detailed explanation and an "executive summary" version in your pre-reading.

6. How do we participate?

There are three major cultural differences in how people prefer to take part in meetings.

Whether differences of opinion are raised *publicly* or *privately*
In US, Australian, or northern European meetings it is normally

expected that differences of opinion will be aired openly and resolved within the meeting.

The open expression and discussion of differences is seen as a positive step toward incorporating different views and developing robust proposals and ideas.

In some Asian and Middle Eastern cultures the surface harmony of the group is much more important and efforts will be made to smooth over differences of opinion in the meeting. If differences of opinion exist, they are better handled privately where the opportunity to lose face is much reduced.

In organizing your cross-cultural meetings, it is wise to give the opportunity for small group and one-to-one discussions on issues of disagreement or to agree to take them outside the meeting.

Be particularly aware of attempts by people who are comfortable with disagreement to force their views on those who wish to avoid conflict. Those cultures and individuals that dislike open conflict may appear to agree in the meeting to prevent further dispute. This agreement is likely to disappear once the meeting has ended.

Whether *everyone* takes part or only the *appropriate people* contribute

In Anglo-American meetings everyone is expected to contribute to discussions, even when they are not particularly knowledgeable in the area being discussed. People feel free to contribute their ideas, even when these conflict with experts or more senior people.

In traditional German corporate cultures it is considered more appropriate only to contribute to issues where you have substantial knowledge or direct involvement in the issue being discussed.

In some Asian cultures there are specific individuals, often of high status or with specific expertise, who are chosen as the right person to respond on behalf of the group.

In cultures where everyone participates, a low level of participation by an individual is a signal of lack of influence or confidence. Quality of contribution is often judged by quantity of contribution.

In cultures where only the proper person contributes, the participation of others can be seen as rude and disrespectful.

Please bear this in mind, especially when you are evaluating people's participation.

Whether participation is *internalized* or *externalized*
For many western cultures the norm is to expect "externalized" forms of participation. These include regular contributions of ideas and opinions, giving signals of paying attention to the speaker (eye contact, non-verbal signals of attention), voting, etc. The more expressive an individual is of their views, the more they are taking part.

For many Asian cultures the norm is to "internalize" contributions. This means showing respect for the speaker by listening quietly and thinking about what is being said. Engaging in open debate is not expected but instead making a serious effort to think through the other person's point of view. The less expressive the individual the more they may be taking part inside.

An understanding of these differences is essential to enable individuals to respect each other's different styles of participation.

Discuss these dimensions in your meeting. Ask people to describe how they prefer to take part and discuss what the implications are of these differences for the way the meeting should run in future. How will you deal with these different expectations? Do your meeting guidelines need to be changed because of this?

International English

International meetings are usually held in a common global or regional corporate language. The most used language for international business meetings is English.

There are some principles below for the good use of "international English"; these are most often abused by native speakers of that language.

> *"Most of us speak 'good enough' business English to communicate, but the native speakers are the hardest to understand, they speak far too fast and use a very complicated vocabulary."*
>
> Supply chain manager, automotive, Mexico

The examples below relate to using international English; the same principles apply if another language such as French, Korean, or Spanish is your corporate language.

If you speak English as a second or third language to a business standard, then your international English is probably already very good. The guidelines below are particularly for native speakers.

It is hard to be prescriptive in this area as it depends very much on the language capabilities and experience in the specific meeting you are working with. You will need to experiment and discuss to find the right level for your meeting.

Good international English principles

- Pace: native speakers often need to slow down the pace at which they speak. This is difficult to describe but we need to find the right balance between being clear and not going so slowly that it sounds patronising
- Clarity: try not to let your thoughts ramble, to change direction in the middle of a sentence or not complete your thought. These twists and turns are extremely difficult to follow in another language
- Vocabulary: use vocabulary that is clear and not unnecessarily complex. Avoid sports and other metaphors that may only be understandable in your own country. It may well be "third down and nine with all to play for" but people without an understanding of American football may not understand what you mean and you may find yourself "batting on a sticky wicket" (ask a British colleague for a translation)
- Humor: amusing stories that are relevant to your point often travel well, but jokes frequently rely on cultural knowledge, assumptions, and understanding. In some cultures humor is not expected in business meetings, in others it is essential – the right balance will depend on who is in the room
- Inclusive: avoid using language or discussing topics that exclude people from other cultures. It may be amusing for people from the dominant culture to discuss what was on TV last night or the latest local politics, news, or "in-joke," but it can be difficult for people who do not share that cultural reference point to contribute. Avoid side discussions among the native

speakers that are too fast or too specialist for others to contribute to

- Breaks: it is quite tiring to concentrate in a second or third language for long periods of time. Allow for more regular breaks and, where possible, allow time where people can work in their local language for a change – either individually or in subgroups

After we introduce ourselves at the beginning of international workshops or keynote speeches, we often ask "How is our English?" It usually gets a laugh as we are native English speakers.

We use this to make a point to ourselves and to other native English speakers in the room that we need to speak good international English. We ask specifically how are the pace, volume, and clarity. Occasionally (even after 20 years of practice in Kevan's case) we still go too fast for an audience and that is great feedback as we can then adapt accordingly.

We also find that international audiences usually appreciate your recognition of this challenge.

If you pay attention to the body language of the audience, you will soon see if they can keep up.

If, during your meeting, you see people are struggling, talk to them at the break and see how you can make things clearer for them. They may wish to sit next to someone who also speaks their language and can help bring them up to speed with things they miss.

Breaking your material up into shorter input sessions with opportunities to discuss and work with the ideas gives time for participants to discuss any problems with their colleagues in local languages.

For more formal international meetings, you can use translators and interpreters but you need to plan for this; you should plan to take twice as long or cover half of the content. This is rarely practical for routine internal meetings.

For your regular meetings, if you think this is a problem, it is worth putting together a short survey that people can use to give feedback to each other on international English.

You can use or adapt the survey below to give feedback to the meeting or to specific speakers. Every individual completes the survey with their own personal evaluation of the meeting or speaker and the meeting facilitator can combine results and lead a discussion on any changes you need to implement.

	Difficult for me 1	2	OK for me 3	4	Good for me 5
Pace					
Clarity					
Vocabulary					
Humor					
Inclusive					
Breaks					

You may find other international English challenges in your specific meeting. Feel free to add them to the feedback form.

Written versus verbal

Many people find it easier to read in another language than to speak in it. Good written materials can improve the participant experience of people operating in a second language.

This is another good reason for well-written pre-reading information circulated in advance of the meeting, as it gives people an opportunity to look up or discuss any topics or vocabulary they do not fully understand.

If you are using slides to support the discussions in the meeting, use them to be clear what you are asking people to do or decide.

9. What time shall we meet?

In global teams, working across time zones introduces an added barrier to communication and cooperation, one more source of complexity and potential confusion and delay.

Two things we can be sure about:

- Time zones are not going to disappear
- There is no convenient time for everybody to attend a global conference or video call – someone is always inconvenienced

A useful tool for scheduling your calls for the most convenient times is http://www.timeanddate.com/worldclock/meeting.html Here you can enter your target locations and it will show you the least inconvenient times to meet.

Here are a few tips for meeting effectively across time zones:

Be aware

It is unforgivable in a global team not to be aware of the local time zones of the people you are working with; it shows a fundamental lack of respect for their time and personal lives.

Be aware of the differences when you schedule live meetings and apologize if you must set an inconvenient time for some participants.

If you are running calls at inconvenient times for some participants, it is even more important to keep them short and relevant.

Avoid them where you can
To decrease the impact of time zones on your team, organize work wherever possible at a local or regional level where time zones can be eliminated or minimized.

Time zones are an opportunity, too
The biggest opportunity for speeding up delivery through time zones is the possibility of continuous 24-hour working. In a global team, you literally have "all the time in the world."

If we organize ourselves, we can take advantage of time zones to deliver faster and at lower cost. We can also offer a 24-hour service to customers and colleagues.

Think relay race not rowing team
It may be more useful to think of teams that work across major differences in time zones as a relay race, where we just hand on the baton at the overlap periods, rather than as a team sport like rowing where everyone is tightly interdependent at all times. There are periods of independence within the region and periods of greater interdependence and possible cooperation in the handover or overlap periods.

Focus on consistent process and communication in the handover period if you plan to work this way across time zones.

Share the pain
While handover across time zones from A to B, from B to C, and then from C to A again can be arranged without much

out-of-hours inconvenience, there is no good time for an audio conference for a global team – someone always suffers.

> *"I was trying to schedule a call recently with a team based in Singapore, London, and San Diego. Five p.m. Thursday in London is midnight in Singapore and 9 a.m. in San Diego. Nine a.m. in Singapore is two in the morning in London and 6 p.m. in San Diego. Whatever I do, one location will be taking part in the middle of the night."*
>
> Customer services director, mobile phones, Ireland

Do not always schedule the call at a convenient time for the headquarters location or where most of the people are. Occasionally rotate the call so everyone gets a share of the inconvenience. It is surprising when you do this how often the call is no longer such a priority.

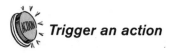 **Trigger an action**

Have you seen any of these behaviors in your meetings? Do you think culture is a factor in improving your meetings? If so, schedule some one-to-one time with your colleagues from other cultures to discuss this. If they agree then put this on the agenda for your next meeting.

 **Discuss this with your team or at your next meeting**

Ask the participants at your meeting to read this chapter or discuss its contents at your meeting and find any of the cultural or other issues mentioned here that they think have an impact on the conduct of your meetings.

Discuss how you can change the way you plan or run your meeting to make it easier for people from a range of cultures to contribute more effectively.

Chapter 12

Running big events and conferences

Actions – apply the techniques to running big events and/or conferences

Target – radically increase the level of participation in your next big event or conference

If it is important to get our everyday meetings right, then it is even more important when we are bringing together large groups of people.

We often deliver keynote sessions or workshops to groups of hundreds of people or more. These might be annual meetings for global organizations, top management programs, or external conferences.

It often seems that more time, money, and attention have been spent on the branding, event logo, and mementos than on creating a great participant experience.

We recently spoke at a conference of 250 people for a global organization, of whom 120 had flown to the meeting from around the world. The rest traveled from within the USA. They stayed in a hotel for three days. With accommodation, meals, travel, and salaries for attendees, by the time the conference began, the organizers had spent over $1 million. The attendees' time alone was equivalent to three person-years of working time.

For an event like this we need to be focused on creating well over $1 million worth of value to make it worthwhile. Instead, the days are often spent sitting listening to presentations with little opportunity to interact.

What objectives are suitable for big events?

In previous chapters, we have used the idea of **star groups** and **spaghetti teams** to define different ways of collaborating. For bigger events, we need to add two more ways of collaborating: communities and networks.

A **cloud community** is a group of people who share a sense of identity that distinguishes them from the broader organization. It implies a shared culture, history, or interest.

This could be a functional community or a community around a shared interest such as project management.

THE PURPOSE OF A COMMUNITY AT WORK IS

- To focus on a domain or topic
- To create and sustain the identity of the community
- To develop the capability of its members through sharing learning and best practice
- To advance their common interests

COMMUNITY MEETINGS AND EVENTS SHOULD FOCUS ON

- Building a sense of common identity
- Sharing values and a sense of social cohesion
- Working together on areas of common interests
- Identifying common practices, the best ways to get things done, the shared sets of approaches, issues, tools, and skills that people need to understand and use to be effective
- Finding expertise and making it visible to the community – who to go to when you have a problem
- Creating opportunities for connection and dialogue and seeing what emerges

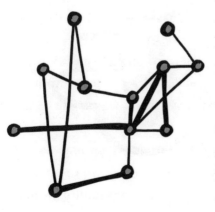

A **purposeful network** is several people who are connected, and related in some way.

They can exchange information and may interact to achieve specific goals. A network is made up of the people and the pattern of connections and interactions between them.

THE PURPOSE OF A NETWORK IS

- To connect and stay connected with a range of people who you may want to engage with more deeply in future
- To maintain these relationships with some form of connection or communication

NETWORK MEETINGS AND EVENTS SHOULD FOCUS ON

- Enabling people to build their networks by meeting relevant new people
- Enabling people to maintain and deepen their networks by having conversations and shared experiences
- Finding opportunities for deeper collaboration

People tend naturally to build networks based on proximity. At big events, we can meet new people and broaden our networks.

However, people tend to sit and socialize with people they already know, so we need to make sure we mix people up and create environments where they meet and work with new people.

It is usually possible to create enough opportunities for networking just by creating free time in a busy agenda and by building in the need to mix and discuss. We will share some ideas on how to do this below.

Most big events are, almost by definition, community events with an additional opportunity for networking. It is important to realize that **these are not teams**; 100 or more people cannot work together at the same time.

At the point at which there is a need to do something – act on common interests, share specific learning, or act in the interest of the community or network – a team or group will often form to get things done.

Start by being clear about your goals for your event. As we have already discussed, information-sharing is not a good objective for a meeting of eight people; so it is certainly not a good objective for a meeting of 200 or more.

The problem of relevance at scale

The fundamental problem with big events is that, as the audience becomes larger, it becomes harder and harder to select a topic that is relevant to everybody.

Take the example of an HR conference in an organization. There may be 100 attendees, all of whom are part of the HR community. They share a sense of identity and belonging to the function.

However, as soon as you get down to the activity of HR and you start to talk about, for example, organization development or learning, then only a subset of this community will find this relevant and interesting.

A good agenda for an event like this might include:

- A recognition of HR's contribution by a senior leader
- Social activities to build a sense of belonging
- Working on the overall HR strategy or deliverables for the year
- Developing new skills that are relevant to everybody, for example ways of working together within HR
- Having a "tradeshow" with booths run by content experts where participants can select the areas they are interested in to attend in small groups to learn what is happening and discuss opportunities to collaborate

- Regular mixing of groups during the day and at breaks and mealtimes to encourage people to broaden their network
- Leaving unstructured time available for people to have conversations

BUILDING THE NETWORK

We were asked by a client some years ago to help facilitate a conference that they had already designed. They were concerned that it lacked interactivity and asked us to help.

They told us that the objective of the event was "networking," which is a great objective given that this was the first time that the global R&D function had met face to face.

Unfortunately, they had already arranged eight presentations where members of the company's executive group wanted to present to this group of 200 R&D people. The topics looked of low relevance to the audience and required little or no participation.

When we pointed this out our client told us that the senior leaders were insistent on doing their presentations; however, they had organized some "team building" for the evening. It emerged that they had organized a trip to the theatre (sit in the dark and do not talk) followed by a formal dinner (only talk to the people immediately next to you).

We advised them that if they had deliberately attempted to develop a networking prevention process, they could not have done a better job.

Giving people an opportunity to build a network is not complicated. We just have to create the opportunity and prevent the natural inclination for people to congregate toward people they already know.

We could do this by:

- Having an activity that forces people to mix early in the agenda – for example an exercise based around finding out people's history, hobbies, or locations
- Changing our table groups regularly, after every break if necessary, so that people get an opportunity to work with a wide range of colleagues
- Regularly changing the way we get people to interact, getting people to do things in pairs, triads, or small groups
- Encouraging informal gatherings during meals and groups – no sit-down meals where you only get to meet two or three people
- Giving people the option to sign up for or choose topics they wish to collaborate on
- Allowing space in the agenda for networking and conversations rather than filling it with presentations

SEEDING THE CLOUD

Instead of forcing cooperation we use big events to "seed the cloud."

At a large meeting of the technical stewardship function in a packaged goods organization we ran a conference that incorporated tradeshows, small round tables with company experts, and whiteboard rooms where people could capture their ideas.

We seeded several topics and themes and got the participants to rotate around, spending as much or as little time as they liked on each topic. The ones who were engaged and motivated and saw real business opportunities signed up to continue to be involved in these topics. Many did not, but the ones who did were willing volunteers who saw real value in collaboration.

This approach tends to be more effective than top-down mandated collaboration.

HOW DO WE CREATE PARTICIPATION IN LARGE AUDIENCES?
Apply our guidelines on designing for participation from Chapter 8 to large events:

- **Focus on the audience**: be clear about your goals for the event and make them and the content relevant to the entire audience. If some of the goals are only relevant to part of the audience, break up the event accordingly
- **For each outcome and process step ask, "What are the participants doing?"**: check what participants are doing at each stage of the process. If the answer is "shutting up and listening to me," then reconsider – give them a role
- **Keep groups small**: in a large event, look for opportunities to break them into smaller groups
  - Use table groups of six to eight people for regular discussions and interactions in the main room
  - Instead of giving eight presentations to 100 people in sequence, turn it into a tradeshow with eight booths where individuals can circulate in smaller groups to discuss the content that is relevant to them

- ○ Rotate the topics: if you have three themes for the day split the group into three and run parallel sessions with three small groups rotating around
- ○ Restrict the time when the large group are all together to the kick-off, breaks and social events
- **Encourage early participation**: get people doing something active in the first four minutes of the event to set your expectations about participation – a networking exercise is a good choice for this
- **Involve people in the generation and creation of materials and ideas** rather than just presenting finished ideas and materials to them. Create opportunities to work in small groups, to add ideas on Post-it notes, to join discussions you are interested in and help develop new ideas and materials
- **Engage all the senses**: brand the room and use music. Encourage movement by getting people to walk around and post things on the walls. Try to keep movement within the main room as every time you move a large group outside the main room, for example to breakout rooms, you lose significant amounts of time.
  - ○ Large numbers of people in the same room also create buzz and energy and prevent people disappearing to make phone calls or answer emails.
  - ○ This means booking a room with enough space for tables and movement.
  - ○ Natural light is also important to maintaining energy levels, particularly for participants who may have traveled recently across time zones and need sunlight to reset their body clocks. Book a venue with lots of windows

- **Make the room layout match the process of the meeting:** if you walk into a room with rows of chairs in a darkened room facing toward a brightly lit stage, this tells you that your role is to shut up and listen. Small round tables encourage participation and group discussion

What to do with all the presentations?

When you bring a lot of people together and it costs a lot of money, it can be tempting to try to fill the agenda with presentations.

It may be one of the few opportunities to get face to face with your colleagues, and senior leaders may be keen to present their strategies, perspectives, and plans. Functional specialists, business unit leaders, and local managers may all have plans and insights to share too.

Unfortunately, listening to these presentations is boring and, if it is just information-sharing, we can achieve the same goal through email. It is not a good use of flying hundreds of people to the same location.

As with all meetings, wherever possible take information-sharing out of the meeting itself.

If you do need people to understand concepts or plans, why not circulate information in advance and run an exercise to check understanding – such as a quiz or taking the development of the idea to the next level. Focus your scarce face-to-face time on what you need to do differently because of this information.

If you have a lot of information to get across and you insist on doing it in a big event, try the tradeshow format so that people can meet the "presenters" in smaller groups, ask them questions and view materials in a more interactive way.

If you still feel that presenting to a large group is the best way to achieve your objectives, why not run a test two or three days after the presentation to see how much people retained? We are confident it will be much less than you expected.

If you focus instead on building your community and networks, people will still be getting value from this for a long time to come.

Going big with virtual meetings

It is not possible to do in-depth collaboration with large numbers of people on a video, WebEx, or conference call.

You can apply the participation principles and examples from Chapter 8 to make a large virtual meeting more engaging, but above a certain size the use of breakouts, etc. to enable participation becomes unwieldy.

Interaction tends to be limited and it can be hard to keep track and respond to large numbers of questions.

Large numbers of participants mean that sharing whiteboards or asking for interaction in anything but the most structured ways is impossible.

In effect the constraints of size and technology force these types of events to focus on star group topics such as broadcasts of information with limited opportunities to interact.

Although this can be an effective way for the individual leading the broadcast to share information, we should still challenge why it is necessary for a large group of attendees to be in the same (virtual) place and time.

An exception could be when you need to share sensitive information to a large group and want to ensure they all receive it at the same time.

If you need to run a meeting like this, keep it short, add in some polls and other interactions to get information or gauge reaction from the audience, and have a colleague monitor questions so that you can respond to the important ones live.

Example: Site "all hands" or "town hall" meetings

One of our clients runs an "all hands" business unit meeting which originally consisted of 200 people sitting in the dark in an auditorium watching presentations from the CEO and other executives on the state of the business. They wanted to make it more interactive and two-way.

The first principle with such a large group is to look for ways to break down the size of the audience – people are much more likely to take part actively in a group of 30 than in one of 200.

The second was to switch to parallel sessions rather than trying to run a sequence of sessions one after the other with the whole audience in one place. By breaking the event up into a series of smaller parallel communication and conversations sessions we could work with group sizes of 30 and seven different topics that people rotated around.

Even smaller group sizes would have been better, but would have been logistically difficult. Every time you move large groups of people you lose a lot of time and focus. The ideal size for creating interaction is around four to six people so even within the groups of 30 we created separate table groups of six people and tried to create activities that enabled discussion around those tables.

Some of the topics were compulsory and everyone needed to attend, while others were voluntary. Giving people the choice to attend or not tends to increase engagement.

Every 45 minutes the groups rotated around a series of workshops or display areas, several of which were designed to get participants' input with Post-it notes and survey tools.

Instead of one-way presentations, the presenters were asked to limit their input to 10–15 minutes and focus on creating conversations with their groups.

People who were unable to get their question answered at the live sessions could post them on wallboards so that after the event we could publish responses.

The small group sizes and regular movement, combined with increased opportunity for participation and conversations, made the event feel much more intimate and lively.

With another of our clients, their CEO was dissatisfied with the traditional "town hall" meetings, where everyone in a location attended. She was expected to travel around the world making presentations to large groups of people with very little feedback from her audience.

We persuaded her to replace this with a much more conversational design. Participants were told that she would be taking questions rather than presenting. Instead of standing at a lectern, she took the stool at the front of the room.

She did this wherever possible with smaller groups and created much more interaction.

After the trip, she told us that not only had she enjoyed the experience much more than the traditional presentations, but that she had also made a note of all the questions that people had asked around the world. She realized that most of the questions that people had asked would not have been in her slide deck. Conversely, nobody had asked questions about most of the content that would have been in the traditional presentation.

She had successfully made the transition from a push style information-giving session to a conversation that was much more relevant to both parties. The feedback from participants was that they felt they had much better access to the CEO and that they enjoyed the discussions far more than the old presentations.

 **Trigger an action**

If you are involved in the design of big events, schedule a note in your diary for when you are planning the next one to discuss and incorporate these ideas.

If you attend big events and think these ideas could improve them, please share this chapter with the people responsible for running the event.

 Discuss this with your event design team

Next time you are designing a large event, share these principles with your design team at an early stage.

Try designing your event around these principles and get feedback from participants on how it compares with previous big events they have attended.

PART 4

Making your meetings flow

• • •

By now you should have a well-designed OPPT meeting plan:

- A clear and relevant set of Outcomes
- Clear Processes to lead you to those outcomes
- The right people and methods of Participation
- A clear view on the Time you want to spend on delivering these outcomes

You should also have:

- Clarity on decision rights and processes in your meeting
- A design that encourages participation and discourages pure information-sharing in the meeting

You have done the hard work and the facilitation of a well-designed meeting should now be relatively easy. However, it is easy to fall back into bad habits and we need to keep people on the track we have designed during the meeting itself.

The next two chapters focus on how we can improve further **during** the running of our meetings and embed a continuous improvement approach into the way we generate and follow up on actions and decisions.

....

- **Chapter 13** – Facilitation tips
- **Chapter 14** – Continuous improvement and follow-up

Chapter 13

Facilitation tips

· ·

 Actions – practice facilitating a meeting that you have designed using the principles in the earlier chapters

 Target – shorten a regular meeting and generate much clearer outcomes and decisions

· ·

Our favorite definition of facilitation is "any activity that makes tasks easy for others."

We prefer to use the title facilitator, rather than chairperson or meeting organizer. The title chairperson is used to describe a person who is in charge. The organizer, to us, is the person who books the room. The facilitator is the person who makes the meeting really work.

The facilitator's role is to lead the group to deliver the planned outcome in the easiest and most effective way possible. Facilitation is a fundamental management skill. If you cannot lead a group to reach an outcome effectively, how can you be a successful manager?

Your OPPT planning has given you several of the tools you need to facilitate effectively.

Being explicit about outcomes and process

The first thing the facilitator should do is introduce each meeting topic using the information from their meeting design.

- What Outcome do we need from this topic?
- What Process will we use to get there?
- How do we expect people to Participate in the process? Including, if appropriate: what decision process will we use?
- How much Time should we give to this?
- It can also be helpful to specify roles and rules.
- Roles: are there specific roles that need to be carried out during the meeting; who will take any notes or record actions, who owns any outcomes, who will lead the discussion?
- Rules: are there any guidelines on participation for the conduct of the meeting; for example, will you ask people to turn off mobile phones and avoid multitasking?

Meeting hopes and fears exercise

To develop your own meeting rules, at the beginning of your next meeting ask participants to reflect on previous meetings they have attended. Ask them to discuss what made particularly good meetings and what made terrible ones.

Ask them to discuss their answers and create a flipchart with two columns, one of their **hopes** for this meeting (what would make this meeting great – things to aspire to) and the other column for their **fears** (what would make this meeting terrible – things to avoid).

Lead a short discussion on what you can do as a facilitator and what they can do as participants to deliver the hopes and prevent the fears. Out of this discussion you will come up with some practical guidelines for preventing some of the common problems with meetings in your organization.

During the meeting, you can display these rules on the wall and refer to them as the meeting progresses. As the rules have been set by the group themselves, they are much more likely to be followed.

If at any point people are not following the rules, then the facilitator can simply point out that these are their rules and ask them how they can resume in a more positive way.

Managing time and focus

It is also the facilitator's role (unless you have a dedicated time-keeper) to keep focus on time and make sure we are covering the planned agenda.

A survey by Atlassian software in the USA found only 53 percent of scheduled meeting time is spent on the agenda items.

As the time allowed for the topic end approaches, give the group some warning that time is running out and then ask them to make an explicit decision whether the topic needs more time or should be ended.

If the participants genuinely need more time, then make sure they understand the consequences for later topics in the agenda. Something will be compressed or missed from the meeting agenda or the meeting will finish late.

It is a good idea to use a flipchart with a timeline on it and Post-it notes for the agenda outcomes. If you have to change the timings, you can move the Post-it notes around and re-plan the rest of the meeting visibly as you go along.

Managing participation

You can use your meeting tick chart again to check who is participating and who is not.

Remember to engage everyone early and regularly.

Go back to your plan on how you wanted people to take part. If you are not getting good levels of participation, then try something different from the ideas in Chapter 8 or ask the group how you could build more participation and energy into the session.

Another good technique is to allocate different roles to different people – have a chairperson, facilitator, content leader for each outcome, scribe, and timekeeper. People with an explicit role naturally feel more engaged.

Dealing with distractions

At some point in most meetings the discussion wanders off into something that is not relevant or is a dead-end. It is hard to stop this happening completely and sometimes it can be fun, but you cannot let this take too much time.

If you have clear outcomes and process you can point to these and ask participants if the discussion is moving them through the process toward the outcome.

You can just ask the question "Is this relevant?" Usually this will bring people back to the topic or you may find out it is relevant in ways you did not realize.

If the distraction is something only of interest to a couple of people, then ask them to continue the discussion after the meeting.

If the discussion is of interest but does not move you toward the outcome of this topic, then capture the issue on a flipchart so you can come back to it later.

Recording outcomes, decisions, and actions

As a facilitator, you should capture any outcomes, decisions, or actions from the meeting.

The best way to do this is on a flipchart which keeps the decisions and actions visible. If you are doing this by webinar you can capture actions on screen. In an audio conference circulate these actions quickly in writing afterwards.

If you are not sure whether people are really committed to their actions, ask them to stand up and record their actions themselves on a flipchart. You will see from the type of words they use how committed they are to actually carrying them out. If the words are vague, ask for clarification and check commitment.

When you reach the end of one topic, **make sure the meeting does not move on to the next one without recording a clear**

outcome. If the meeting is unable to reach the outcome planned, make a note of why so you can improve your planning for the next meeting.

At face-to-face meetings you can produce and copy a hand-written version at the end of the meeting or photograph the actions flipchart and circulate it to attendees straight away if you prefer not to type it up.

> *"At our leadership meeting the CEO writes a handwritten one-page briefing of the results of the management meeting each week. We each take a copy and use it as the basis for briefing our own people – that way messages are always consistent."*
>
> Manufacturing director, drinks, UK

At the end of the meeting, review the outputs on your flipchart and for each one ask:

• Who is responsible for implementing this?
• When will it be done by?
• Who needs to be informed about this?

If it is a small number of individuals who have all the actions, challenge whether this is acceptable.

If individuals regularly do not have any actions at all, then it is worth considering whether they need to be at future meetings.

Set a clear expectation that you will be reviewing their actions at the next meeting; see the next chapter for more on this.

Do not forget to check whether the type and quality of actions generated were a good return on your investment of time and effort in the meeting.

A good final question is "Given what we achieved – was this a good use of your time?" If it was not, then discuss what would make better use of the time at the next meeting.

Making decision points explicit

Meetings can sometimes drift into an apparent decision. After long discussion, people stop talking, they assume a decision is made and move on to the next point. This is usually a recipe for confusion and poor decision implementation.

As a facilitator, when you think the decision has been made, make it explicit.

Ask questions like, "So, have we made a decision?" And if so, "What is it?"

Capture the decision in writing on the flipchart and ask the group to confirm that your description is correct.

If you doubt whether people are really committed to the decision a useful technique is to carry out a commitment check.

Ask everyone to take a piece of paper each and write a number on it that reflects how committed they are to the implementation of this decision. A score of 1 means no intention of implementing it at all. A score of 10 means they are fully committed to making it happen, come what may.

Ask everyone to hold up their paper at the same time. If the average score is less than seven you do not have a commitment. If the score is low for some (or all) individuals you can ask why, and what would improve it for them.

You can also tell you haven't got a proper decision if no individual will claim ownership or give a completion date.

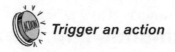 **_Trigger an action_**

Review this chapter and put together a plan for how you will facilitate your next meeting. Do not try to do everything at once, begin by using OPPT, setting up meeting rules and expectations, and recording outcomes.

 Discuss this with your team or at your next meeting

- Discuss with your participants how you plan to run your meeting
- Develop some agreed meeting rules
- Try the techniques above and ask for feedback on how they have an impact on the meeting

Chapter 14

Continuous improvement and follow-up

 Actions – establish a continuous improvement process in your meetings by reviewing past actions

 Target – improve the implementation of decisions and actions taken in your meeting

One of the oldest and most effective meetings practices is to keep a note of actions and decisions made at the meeting and then, at the next meeting, review whether the actions were completed or decisions implemented. It is very simple and obvious but it is surprising how few meetings actually do this.

Just having this process in place will significantly increase the probability that people have implemented their actions; if not, they need to explain why.

If any individuals with actions from the last meeting are not attending the meeting, then the meeting facilitator should check the progress of these actions before the meeting and report back on their behalf.

An old saying in manufacturing is "expect what you inspect." If you do not pay any attention to whether your actions are implemented, then you are signalling that you do not think this is important.

If actions have not been completed, then they should carry over to the next meeting and the individual concerned should come along and explain why not.

"We have a stand-up production meeting where we review outstanding quality problems every morning. All actions are displayed on a large magnetic board and, so long as an individual had an action live on the board, they must turn up every morning to explain what is happening with it. As the meeting is at 8 a.m. every day and is very public, people tend to complete their actions very quickly."

Production supervisor, packaged goods, USA

This is effectively a continuous improvement process for your meetings outcomes.

If you keep a record of your meetings actions and check whether they were implemented, you can quickly see whether creating these actions was worthwhile. If they are not being implemented, why is this? Is it that they are poor quality actions, or do you not really have the authority to make those types of recommendations, or is it that you need to improve the implementation of your decisions?

If some specific participants are regularly not following up on their actions, you need to speak to them about why and, if necessary, replace them in your meeting.

Teams that employ this continuous improvement approach

often find that they need to do a better job of communicating their actions, so check if this has been one of the problems.

Continuous improvement check

To keep your meetings from slipping back into bad habits and to keep them evolving to cope with new topics, participants, and technologies, it is essential to get into the habit of continuous improvement.

At the end of your regular meeting, webinar, or call ask participants the following questions, or come up with some of your own (you can do this on a flipchart, online poll, or follow-up email).

1. Was this meeting a good use of your time?
2. What specifically would have made it (even) better?
3. Did you receive the outcomes and process for this meeting far enough in advance to prepare?
4. Were the right participants in the meeting to achieve the planned outputs? If not who should or should not have been there?
5. Did we stick to time?
6. Were the topics relevant to you? If not, which specific ones were not?
7. Did the process of the meeting allow you to take part as you wanted to? If not, what would have made it better for you?
8. Did the meeting focus on collaboration, decisions, and discussion rather than information-giving?
9. Were the decisions and actions from the meeting recorded and communicated?

10. Did we review the implementation of actions from the previous meeting?
11. Did we achieve the outcomes we planned?

If you act on any areas where people are dissatisfied you will continuously refine the conduct, content, and quality of your meetings.

Younger participants in particular value this constant feedback, input of their ideas, and improvement. The more opportunities you can create to encourage immediate feedback and act on this, the faster you will improve.

You should do this at least once a year with all your regular meetings.

Make your meeting OPPT-ional

Now you have re-engineered your meetings to be much more relevant and engaging, here is a real test of whether they are actually a great use of people's time.

Make your meetings optional. If people choose to attend, then this is telling you that they value the meeting. If they choose not to attend they are telling you that this meeting is not as useful as alternative ways of spending their time.

If people opt out of your meeting, then you should first consider that perhaps they are right. It may be that they are not the right participants or that your meeting is not as valuable to them as you think.

If you have truly designed a successful OPPT meeting, then people should choose to opt in.

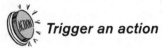 *Trigger an action*

Look back at the actions of previous meetings and see how well you have done in implementing them. If they haven't been implemented take some time to find out why – is there a pattern? Set up a meeting log to record future outcomes and check how well they have been followed.

There are several useful action tracking or project management apps such as Trello that you can use to manage actions visibly and collectively.

 *Discuss this with your team or at your next meeting*

- Use the continuous improvement questions above to conduct an audit of your meeting
- Evaluate how well your decisions and actions have been implemented
- Discuss any areas of improvement with the participants
- Update the way you plan your meetings

PART 5

Embedding the Change

• • •

When we ask our training course participants how to run the perfect meeting, most can give a good answer. However, when we ask them how often they attend meetings that are run this way the answer is "Almost never."

Many of the ideas in this book are simple common sense. However, to paraphrase Frank Lloyd Wright, "There is nothing more uncommon than the consistent application of common sense."

As we saw in Part 1, there are many corporate cultural issues contributing to the symptom of too many meetings.

There is also a huge amount of inertia and the legacy of poor meetings practice to overcome.

In this part of the book we will look at how you embed change and overcome resistance to the new ways of working you are introducing.

Chapter 15

Embedding the change and overcoming resistance

Actions – identify and deal with any specific objections to this new way of working

Target – maintain your improvement, overcome resistance to change and pressure to fall back into attending unnecessary and badly run meetings

If you have followed the actions and met your targets from the previous chapters, you have now cut out unnecessary topics and participants, planned your meetings using OPPT, and are running significantly fewer, better face-to-face and virtual meetings.

By now you have probably already met some resistance to your changes.

Some of this is simply inertia. It is hard and takes energy to change established routines and habits. Other aspects of resistance emerge because meetings have meaning beyond just performing a task or reaching a decision.

- People can respond personally or feel upset if you do not attend their meetings or invite them to yours – even if it is for good reasons
- Individuals who are used to regular meetings may feel a loss of involvement or community – even though they added nothing to the conduct of the meeting and probably used to complain about it being boring
- Your corporate culture may encourage regular meetings and consensus decision-making – even where they do not add value

It is also not enough to improve meetings "once and for all"; circumstances and meeting members change, so we need to embed the habit of continuous improvement in our meeting practices to ensure our meetings will evolve and improve over time.

The series of actions in this book were designed around well-researched change management principles to keep each step simple and to focus on changing one thing at a time. It is critical to embed each of these steps into your habitual way of working, to do it without thinking rather than to have to consciously plan it each time.

In this chapter, we will focus on some of the common signs of resistance to change and what to do about them by:

- Understanding some of the sources of resistance to change
- Embedding the recommended practices in your habits and routines
- Encouraging you to evangelize this approach with your colleagues
- Showing you how to overcome some common objections

Understanding some of the sources
of resistance to change

It can be uncomfortable and tiring to do things differently. It is much easier to continue doing things the same way as it doesn't require thought or effort. Overcoming this inertia to make a change in the first place can be difficult.

In meetings, however, we have a compelling business case and a strong personal motivation in cutting out unnecessary and boring meetings. By making this explicit we can build the energy for change. We meet very few people who are satisfied with the number or the conduct of their meetings.

The lure of saving a day a week spent in unnecessary and frustrating meetings gives a strong impetus to change.

That's why we start the campaign by building the business case for change, and why we break the campaign down into a series of simple actions and targets that you can implement one at a time. If you try to make many changes all at once, each of them is less likely to be achieved.

It is also why we encourage you to be explicit and discuss what you are doing with your meeting participants. If people understand the process and buy into the outcomes from the start, they are much more likely to implement the change.

If we can embed these new practices into our way of working, then inertia works in our favor by making sure we continue to apply them forever.

Popular self-help books suggest it takes 28 days to change a habit, but academic research shows wide variations depending on your personality and the type of habit you are trying to change. It may take you months to embed new behaviors, so you need to concentrate until they become second nature.

There may also be challenges with your corporate culture: assumptions about involvement, consensus, and teamwork may lead you to involve more people than are strictly necessary. It can be tough to make a major change that is not consistent with your culture. If this is your problem, then you might ask someone in the part of your organization that is responsible for organizational change or organization development for support, or contact Global Integration to discuss how we can support this change initiative. You can contact us at meetings@global-integration.com

You may need support from your senior leaders and active modelling of the change from role models in your business to really make it stick at scale across the organization.

However, please do not use this as an excuse for not doing something yourself! You can start by improving your own meetings and use this to demonstrate the opportunity to your colleagues.

Embedding the recommended practices in your habits and routines

Link the principles from this book to trigger events in your daily work, so that you establish new habits. For example, when you receive a meeting invitation, think **No outcomes, no meeting**; do not accept without thinking.

If you are sitting in a meeting and it lacks relevance, turn to the meeting leader and ask, "Is this spaghetti?"

Use the meeting planner to design in the principle "if there is no outcome or participation, we do not need a meeting." Decline to attend meetings that are not planned this way.

If you get everyone in your team or regular meeting a copy of this book and systematically work together through the chapters, then they will understand what you are trying to achieve. You can then can hold each other to account for maintaining the standards. Social pressure is an important element of changing habits.

It may be worth revisiting some of the chapters that have been particularly challenging or running communication campaigns around particular issues. For example, try running a "Say no to meetings month" with your team from time to time.

Evangelize

If this approach to meetings has worked for you, try to spread it to your colleagues. It is hard to make a significant cultural change on your own. The more widely shared and applied the ideas are throughout your organization, the easier it will be for you to continue to run your meetings this way.

If you have a good result personally with this approach, just imagine what it would mean if these practices were rolled out to your whole organization.

Dealing with objections

Here are a few of the reasons that people have given us for resisting a reduction in meetings, and some ideas about how to overcome them.

"People complained about our meetings then complained about me cancelling them. I think people just got used to how bad they were and could not see an alternative way to feel involved. Now we have a lot more one-to-ones and informal lunch gatherings, it seems to work."

Site manager, consulting, Belgium

- **We have terrible meetings but the by-products are useful**: when we cancel meetings, or ask participants not to attend, they may agree that the meeting was not useful, but feel they are missing some of the positive by-products by not attending. People often attend meetings to improve their visibility or build their network, even if the content is not relevant

The solution to this is to work directly on the by-products. Networking is useful and visibility is important in most organizations but sitting bored in irrelevant meetings is not a suitable process for improving either of them. If people need networking organize open days, social events, or "meet and greets" where people can expand their network and meet new people.

You can improve visibility by arranging lunches with senior managers or by identifying relevant meetings that individuals can attend. Visibility is not a good reason to continue to attend unnecessary meetings.

- **We value involvement or community**: if meeting leaders cancel regular team meetings where the topics are mainly one-to-one, or of limited relevance, they often experience a backlash from team members who claim to feel a lack of "involvement" or belonging

This is a valid objection. People do like to know what's going on and have a chance to meet to maintain a sense of community and relationships. If this is the real objective of your meeting, it may be better to organize a lunch conversation or evening social event. If you do have a meeting, then it should focus on common learning, celebrating success and socializing, rather than on the presentations and information-giving that are usually the focus of activity-based meetings.

- **I like to know what is going on**: in any meeting or team, you will often find one or more individuals who have a high tolerance and desire for information. They like to know what's going on and think it is a good use of their time to be copied on every email and to attend every meeting. This can be a sign of insecurity or it may just be a historical expectation based on how things have been done in the past

In today's increasingly connected organization it is not possible and perhaps not even desirable to keep in touch with everything. Have a conversation with individuals who want too much information about a realistic expectation of how much involvement you and they can afford.

Be careful not to run your meetings at the level that satisfies these few "information junkies" and sends everyone else to sleep.

- **You do not come to my meetings, you hate me**: some people react personally if you do not attend their meetings, even if they aren't relevant. Many see it as an indication of disloyalty or dislike or they may think it undervalues their contribution. If these are senior managers this can be a serious problem

It could be helpful to be able to share your learning from this book with them and perhaps get them a copy of their own. If they understand the purpose and the process they are less likely to take it personally.

You should also take care to frame your actions as part of a deliberate intent to improve ways of working and be more effective.

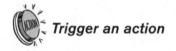

Trigger an action

If you are experiencing resistance to reducing the number or improving the quality of your meetings, take some time to consider why this is and what you can do about it.

Discuss this with your team or at your next meeting

- If resistance emerges, be explicit about it – discuss it and use the information in this book to help defuse the resistance
- Brief your meeting or team members on how to communicate what you are doing so others will understand the

reasons for your actions. This helps prevent misunder-
standings or misinterpretations
- Encourage the resisters to read this book so they are
exposed to the same ideas

Chapter 16

Conclusions

If you have completed your actions and reached your target in each of the chapters of this book you will already have made a significant reduction in the number of meetings you attend and an improvement in the quality of those that remain.

- Killing unnecessary meetings and topics and removing unnecessary participants can radically reduce the number and length of your meetings and slim down the number of people who attend. This is usually a win for everyone
- More effective meeting planning enables you to make better use of your remaining meetings and focus them on delivering clear outcomes and higher levels of engagement
- Effective facilitation of the meeting makes meetings more engaging to participate in and delivers clearer results faster

Here is an opportunity to go back to your original business case and see what kind of impact this has had on the time you spend in meetings and your satisfaction with them.

You may want to repeat any surveys you did at the beginning to collect this information. The opportunity in applying the ideas in this book is to save yourself a day per week of unnecessary meetings.

You should find a huge return on your investment in buying and reading this book. Meetings are expensive and the ideas in this book are inexpensive to apply, usually requiring no more investment than a bit of your time.

As we have seen, changing your meetings culture can seem like a relatively simple task but there is tremendous inertia and legacy expectation based on decades of poor quality meetings. There can also be corporate cultural assumptions that make meetings hard to escape from.

You may need to go back through the chapters of this book from time to time to prevent a slide back into poor meetings practice, or you may need to consider a broader company-wide program to drive out poor quality meetings.

Remember to use the continuous improvement questions in Chapter 12 to drive regular discussions on how you could improve your meetings even further.

If you need any further help with implementing these ideas through consulting, coaching, training your in-house facilitators, or online, webinar, or face-to-face training, our contact details are below.

The quality of meetings is within your control. If you do nothing you will continue to waste a day a week. Everyone else in your meetings is just as frustrated as you are.

All the value of the ideas in this book come from their implementation. We wish you luck with applying the ideas and would love to hear about your experiences.

Good luck.

Kevan Hall and Alan Hall
meetings@global-integration.com
www.global-integration.com

About Global Integration

We inspire and enable people to succeed in increasingly connected matrix, virtual, and global organizations.

We do this in three key areas:

1. Consulting and support for senior leaders driving organizational transformation
2. Building the capabilities and confidence needed to lead, cooperate, and succeed in a complex, matrix, virtual, and global environment
3. Driving sustainable change in ways of working and people practices (such as the way we meet, decide, and travel) to create a truly connected organization

This book gives you an introduction to our approach in just one topic in the third area – fundamentally changing the way we meet.

In this specific area, we can help you kill bad meetings through consulting, training workshops, or providing skilled observers and coaches to work with your most important meetings and leaders.

We can also train and license your in-house facilitators to use this approach.

Since 1994 we have trained over 100,000 people in the skills required to succeed in complex organizations in over 300 of the world's leading companies in more than 40 countries.

We deliver our services globally either face to face, by webinar, through online learning, or with blended solutions incorporating elements of all three.

You can engage with us in your own region through our offices in Europe, the Americas, and Asia.

Read our other books: *Making the Matrix Work: How Matrix Managers Engage People and Cut Through Complexity*, and *Speed Lead: Faster, Simpler Ways to Manage People, Projects and Teams in Complex Companies*, both by Kevan Hall.

Find out more or contact us at www.global-integration.com where you can also sign up to receive our monthly insights.

Connect with our Global Integration page or our Matrix Management group on LinkedIn or follow us on Twitter @GlobalInteg or @killbadmeetings

ALSO BY KEVAN HALL

SPEED LEAD

Faster, Simpler Ways to Manage People,
Projects and Teams in Complex Companies

"We want our companies to be faster, simpler, and easier to run – this
refreshing blend of challenging ideas and practical tools shows us how"
Karl Kahofer, Group President Europe
and Asia Pacific, Rubbermaid/IRWIN

Today's managers waste an estimated 40 per cent of their time on unnecessary cooperation, communication, and control. Old-fashioned management skills are too expensive and slow to use in today's complex companies. When great companies grow they become more complex. This complexity starts to undermine what made the company successful: the organization slows down, it is more difficult to get things done, and it becomes a less satisfying workplace.

Contrary to current leadership wisdom, *Speed Lead* advises to: celebrate the end of teams where you don't need them; abolish meetings of the bored; take control of the "crack-berry" and don't be a 24-hour control freak; expect more from your people and lead a lot less; make "good-enough" decisions; and, don't let diversity be a diversion – share practices, not values.

ISBN 978 1 85788 374 9